INTRODUCTION TO EAST ROMAN (BYZANTINE) COINAGE

by

JOHN F. LHOTKA, M.D., Ph D

SANFORD J. DURST
NUMISMATIC PUBLICATIONS
NEW YORK, N.Y.

ISBN No. 0 - 942666 - 53 - 4
LC No. 88 - 72080

Published and Distributed by
Sanford J. Durst
29-28 41st Avenue
Long Island City, NY 11101

Originally Published
in the
Numismatist
of the
American Numismatic Association

PREFACE

When the author became interested in the coinage of the East Roman Empire in the early fifties, there simply were no available references to aid the beginner. All were out of print. Unless one had access to one of the large numismatic libraries, the only means of learning about the series was picking up bits and pieces from other references. Fortunately for the writer, a copy of Goodacre was obtained on loan and a bit later, the Wroth catalogues became available. This lack of readily available information about Byzantine coins in English (or any language for that matter) influenced the author, when he had amassed sufficient information, to prepare this monograph in an effort to fill an obvious gap in basic numismatic data. The initial work, when finished, appeared in the Numismatist serially and then with the second work on common bronzes was combined under the original title, *Introduction to East Roman Coinages*, and released as an ANA reprint. Then as so often happens in the numismatic world, the Byzantine series, as they say, caught fire, and in a fairly short time reprint editions of the Wroth British Museum catalogues, an updated Goodacre, the old warhorse Sabatier, the 1930 Ratto catalogue, and even Tolstoi appeared on the market. Incidentally, it is amazing how few people know that the author of *War and Peace* was an avid numismatist and authority on the Byzantine coinage. Then in short date, original works appeared incorporating research of the more recent years such as the little volume by Rynearson, the volumes by Whitting and Grierson, and of course the priced catalogue of David Sear. Probably the most important publication was the appearance of the Dumbarton Oaks catalogues edited by Bellinger and Grierson. These texts (3 volumes in 5 parts to date) are now the definitive reference to Byzantine coinage. The question that obviously arises is, "Why with all of these publications is it of value to reprint this particular work?" In the author's opinion, and happily in that of others, it is simply that this is the only reference aimed at the basic collector and provides a stepping stone to the more advanced references. Using the information in this book, a collector can learn to identify a common coin, determine the issuing ruler, the denomination, and if possible, the mint of origin and even the year of issue. Once the collector has mastered this information, he can then proceed to more advanced texts. However, the author recommends that if possible, the collector should try and locate a Goodacre so he or she can savor the tale of empire that accompanies the coin lists in that book. It will increase one's enjoyment and interest in this fascinating series. It is one of a kind.

John F. Lhotka
March 1989

TABLE OF CONTENTS

INTRODUCTION TO EAST ROMAN COINAGE
PART I. BYZANTIUM

One of the most fascinating numismatic series, and probably one of the most neglected in the United States, is that of the East Roman or Byzantine Empire. This is partially due to the lack of adequate references to the series and also probably due to a certain lack of beauty or artistic value of the coins themselves. However, to anyone who has read Gibbon's Decline and Fall of the Roman Empire, there is an interest in this group that is rarely found in any other numismatic series. It is possible with these coins to trace the rise and fall of one of the greatest stories of empire ever known to the Christian world, rivaling in many respects its spiritual father, the old Roman Empire of Augustus and Trajan. From a religious standpoint alone the series has intense interest. Probably no other nation ever so completely lived in a religious atmosphere, the art, the books, and even the political attitude of the Byzantines was steeped in an intense, and to some extent fanatical, religious feeling. This is reflected in the coinage which in the earlier days presented the cross and the christogram as common reverse types. Then the intense bitterness of the iconoclastic controversy of the eighth century drove the religious symbols from the currency, only to have them return in full strength by the Comnenian period. In the final days of the empire the religious fervor became extreme as if the last remnants of the Byzantine nation felt their only salvation lay in the Almighty. This intense feeling, in fact, helped the final ruin of the nation when it was split between the Catholicism of the last of the Paleologi and the Orthodox spirit of the bulk of the people at a time when unity was the only chance of salvation.

In the earlier part of this century and in the latter part of the nineteenth century a number of good texts were issued on Byzantine coins. The two most popular ones in English are those of Wroth (British Museum Catalogues) and Goodacre (published by Spink and Son). However, at the present, these are almost impossible to obtain and the average collector is unable to find any adequate basic reference on the Byzantine series unless he has access to one of the large numismatic libraries. This complete absence of a basic reference to the coinage of the Byzantine empire, coupled with a desire to present this fascinating coinage to the average collector, decided the preparation of this paper. This is not an original work but more of a compilation of earlier works, simplified, and reorganized for the collector who has no experience with Byzantine coins. A general knowledge of the Roman coinage is assumed but is not necessary to understand the general approach of this work.

In the various tables contained in this paper listing obverse legends, it will be noted that some of the emperors mentioned in the historical outline are not listed. In such cases, the emperor in question was not known to have issued coins in his own name (like ALEXIUS II or JOHN VI) or he died before he was able to strike coins even though he may have been depicted on the reverse of his predecessor's coinage (like STAURACIUS).

The Eastern Roman Empire struck coins in gold, electrum, silver, billon, and bronze, the gold and bronze ones being the most commonly available at the present. In contrast to the profuse silver coinage of the earlier empire, silver Byzantine coins are decidedly scarce and frequently are far more expensive than gold coins of the same ruler.

The solidus, weighing about 68 grains, was the standard gold coin struck in the early days of the eastern empire, being the continuation of the denomination introduced into Roman currency in the Constantinian era. With little change in weight or appearance, this denomination was continued into the eleventh century when it assumed a cup shaped or "scyphate" form and became known as the "nomisma." These are the coins so frequently referred to in the western literature of that time as "bezants" and which were accepted as valid currency throughout all of Europe in the absence of an adequate western European coinage. The smaller divisions of the solidus, the semissis (one-half) and the tremissis (one-third), were struck up until the tenth century. During the reigns of the Paleologi, gold became quite scarce and was replaced by the silver and bronze coinage. After Manuel II, essentially no gold coins were struck at Constantinople.

As with the solidus, the initial silver coin struck by the Byzantines was a continuation of the Constantinian siliqua and persisted as such until the reign of Justin I, when it was supplanted by a very small silver coin. The hexagram, weighing about 100 grains, was introduced by Heraclius and persisted until replaced by the miliaresion in the reign of Constantine V. The miliaresion was quite distinctive being thin and flat with an inscription containing the imperial name on the obverse, rather than a bust, and usually a cross potent on the reverse. The silver began to assume the scyphate form in the reign of Constantine IX although both flat and scyphate coins continued to be struck in some reigns. In the last days of the empire, Manuel II in an attempt to reform the coinage abandoned the scyphate form and issued flat silver and bronze coins.

The bronze coinage of the early eastern empire also was a continuation of the Roman types of the fourth century, both in size and appearance. The classical reverse legends such as SALVS AVGGG, CONCORDIA AVGGG, etc., were standard, while the emperor's bust was still present on the obverse as it had been for hundreds of years. However, Anastasius I reformed the coinage by dividing the solidus, which itself was not affected, into six thousand theoretical units called nummia. The smaller coins were then struck in fractions of this amount. While this did not seriously change the silver currency, it did alter the appearance of the bronze coinage. The time honoured reverse legends and types were abandoned and replaced with symbols indicating the value of the coin in nummia. Forty nummia (M) was the largest denomination struck in bronze while five nummia (E) was the smallest. In addition to these, coins were also struck in the values of thirty (XXX), twenty (K), sixteen (IS), twelve (IB), ten (I), eight (H), and six (S) nummia. The Carthage mint in some cases did not use the standard symbols but used instead the Roman numerals to indicate ten (X), twenty (XX), and forty (XXXX) nummia pieces. These reverse inscriptions continued well into the iconoclastic period of the empire when the bronze coins began to resemble the gold and silver in reverse types. In the later empire, after the settlement of the iconoclastic controversy, ecclesiastical types became standard for denominations in all metals.

During the reign of John I in the tenth century, the so-called "anonymous bronze" series was introduced in which the obverse contained a bust of Christ with an inscription, usually a variation of "EMMANOVHA," while the reverse contained a "King of Kings" inscription usually arranged around a cross. The imperial name was lacking creating some difficulty in properly attributing these coins. The Cherson mint, however, continued to strike coins bearing the imperial name (usually a monogram) long after the other mints were striking only the anonymous types. This type of coinage supplanted all other forms of bronze coinage, until well into the eleventh century when attributed coins were again issued. There is some question as to when attributed coins were again struck, some believing that anonymous coinage ceased about the time of Constantine IX, others believing that it continued into the Comnenian reigns. The details of this anonymous coinage is beyond the scope of this paper and those interested should consult recognized texts on Byzantine currency and the many papers published on this subject.

A uniform arrangement has been adopted in this paper in approaching the study of Byzantine coinage. The thousand years of the Empire's existence have been divided into seven more or less arbitrary periods, each named for convenience sake after a dynasty that ruled the Empire during either all or part of the era. After a brief historical outline of each period, its coinage is discussed in general as to the prevalent types and inscriptions followed by a list of representative obverse and reverse legends. Except in a general way, no attempt has been made to individually differentiate the coins struck in precious metals from those struck in bronze since the purpose of this paper is not to distinguish individual coins but to acquaint the reader with Byzantine coinage in general. Those interested in more detailed studies on East Roman Coinage are recommended to the fine texts mentioned previously by Goodacre and Wroth.

It is hoped that the tables given in this paper will assist the average collector in identifying the Byzantine coins he may possess at least as to ruler, if not denomination, and will simultaneously offer him a basic source of information on this interesting series that has been lacking in recent years.

HISTORICAL OUTLINE — THEODOSIAN PERIOD

The Theodosian dynasty was established by the last emperor to rule over a unified Roman nation, THEODOSIUS I (379-395 A.D.), the man who has given the name to this first Byzantine Period. Oddly enough, Theodosius himself is not considered in our tables, since his coinage is well covered in texts on the late Roman series. At his death, the empire was divided between his two weak sons, HONORIUS in the west, and his older brother, the ineffectual

ARCADIUS (395-408 A.D.), the first true Byzantine ruler. Arcadius was a weak ruler but with the aid of his counselors and generals was able to pass a still unified nation to his young son

THEODOSIUS II (408-450 A.D.) who ruled first with the advice of the Praetorian Prefect Anthemius and later under the direction of his extremely capable sister, PULCHERIA. Pulcheria and his wife EUDOCIA shared between them the control of the emperor with the sister eventually obtaining the upper hand. Toward his death, Theodosius was directed by his eunuch Chrysaphius. On his death in 450 A.D., Theodosius left no direct successor so his sister Pulcheria married and elevated to the throne,

MARCIAN (450-457 A.D.) a Thracian soldier. After a fairly able administration considering the times, Marcian died, preceded by his empress,

Fig. 1.   Small bronze coin of Arcadius.
Fig. 2.   Tremissis of Eudoxia (Constantinople mint).
Fig. 3.   Solidus of Marcian.
Fig. 4.   Tremissis of Leo I.

and again the throne lacked a legitimate successor. The commanding general, the Alan Aspar, unable to succeed to the throne himself because of religious differences, nominated a Dacian soldier

LEO (457-474 A.D.) who founded the Leonine dynasty. Leo, noting that the Alan Aspar would not be content unless he were a complete puppet, arranged for his removal by an Isaurian soldier, Tarasicodissa, whom he married to his daughter ARIADNE. After his death, Leo was succeeded by his sickly grandson

LEO II (474 A.D.) who made his father, now called Zeno, his imperial colleague. Leo died shortly after his succession and his father

ZENO (474-491 A.D.) became emperor. Zeno's reign was turbulent and he was troubled with two pretenders, BASILISCUS who was married to Zeno's sister, ZENONIS, and later by LEONTIUS. Zeno was able to put down both rebellions in spite of the fact that during the first rebellion (476-477 A.D.) Basiliscus was able to control his capital. At his death, no legitimate successor was available so Ariadne, using the example of Pulcheria, married a worthy but elderly soldier, Anastasius I, and elevated him to the throne, ending the Theodosian period.

SUMMARY OF THE COINAGE OF THE THEODOSIAN PERIOD

The bust of the emperor, diademed or helmeted, is practically always on the obverse, generally facing the right although in the later years of the period full faced busts became common. The full facing busts are more commonly found on the larger denomination coins, especially the solidus.

The reverses of all denominations present the same series of stylized pictorializations associated with the Roman coinage of the late fourth century. The emperor, usually vanquishing an enemy or holding standards of victory, is a common reverse in all denominations. Personifications of Roma, usually seated in armor holding a small Victory, and Victory, winged and walking to right or left and frequently carrying a standard, are common during this era. In the earlier days of the period when a western emperor still existed, he is often shown, especially on the solidus, seated on the reverse next to his eastern colleague. On the smaller coins, the christogram, the cross (usually potent), and the imperial monogram are popular reverse designs.

Mint marks are found on the exergual space of the reverse. It should be noted that while the western empire retained its authority, coins were struck at western mints in the name of the eastern emperor so that coins of Treves or Milan may bear the bust of the eastern ruler. A list of mint marks used during this and several subsequent periods is given in the appendix.

HISTORICAL OUTLINE — JUSTINIANEAN PERIOD

ANASTASIUS I (491-518 A.D.) after a mildly troubled reign died childless leaving the empire financially and militarily in the best shape it had been in for many years. He was succeeded by the commander of the palace guard, a rough illiterate Illyrian soldier

JUSTIN I (518-527 A.D.) who was able to bribe his election as ruler with money entrusted him for the election of another. Justin, in spite of his inability to read or write beyond the barest essentials, was able to keep the empire in fairly good condition, until in 527 when he associated his well educated, intelligent, but somewhat thankless nephew

JUSTINIAN I (527-565 A.D.) with him in the government. Justin died shortly afterward leaving Justinian as sole emperor. Justinian was an ambitious man who felt keenly the state of his empire when compared to the glories of the past. He resolved to reconquer the western provinces, and aided by his brilliant generals, Belisarius and Narses, was able to actually re-establish some authority in the west. He had several disturbances at home, particularly the great "Nika Revolt" which he quelled only through the courage of his famous wife, Theodora. After his death, Justinian in turn was succeeded by his nephew, the unpredictable

JUSTIN II (565-578 A.D.) who proceeded to lose many of the conquests his uncle had made during his long reign. Much of Justin's misrule was caused by his strong minded wife, SOPHIA (who is shown with him on some coins), but fortunately for the empire in a lucid moment he adopted one of his favorite generals, the count of the palace guard

REPRESENTATIVE OBVERSE LEGENDS OF THE
THEODOSIAN PERIOD

Arcadius, 395-408
   1. DN ARCADIVS PF AVG
Aelia Eudoxia (wife of Arcadius)
   1. AEL EVDOXIA AVG
Theodosius II, 408-450
   1. DN THEODOSIVS PF AVG
Aelia Eudocia (wife of Theodosius II)
   1. AEL EVDOCIA AVG
Marcian, 450-457
   1. DN MARCIANVS PF AVG
Aelia Pulcheria (wife of Marcian)
   1. AEL PVLCHERIA AVG
Leo I, 457-474
   1. DN LEO PF AVG
   2. DN LEO PERPET AVG
Aelia Verina (wife of Leo I)
   1. AEL VERINA AVG
Leo II, 474 (with step-father, Zeno)
   1. DN LEO ET ZENO PP AVG
Aelia Ariadne (mother of Leo II, wife of Zeno)
   1. AEL ARIADNE AV
Zeno, 474-491
   1. DN ZENO PERP AVG
Basiliscus, 476-477 (usurper in reign of Zeno)
   1. DN BASILISCVS PP (PERP) AVG
Aelia Zenonis (wife of Basiliscus)
   1. AEL ZENONIS AVG
Leontius, 484-488 (usurper in reign of Zeno)
   1. DN LEONTIVS PERP AVG

REPRESENTATIVE REVERSE LEGENDS

1. CONCORDIA AVGG (G)
2. CONCORDIA MILITVM
3. GLORIA REIPVBLICAE
4. GLORIA ROMANORVM
5. SALVS AVGGG
6. SALVS REIPVBLICAE
7. VICTORIA AVGGG
8. VICTORIA AVGVSTORVM
9. VIRTVS EXERCITI
10. VIRTVS ROMANORVM (AVGG)
11. VOT V (X) MVLT X (XV, XX)
12. VRBS ROMA

13. The Christogram

14. Cross Potent —

Fig. 5. 40 nummia piece of Anastasius I (Constantinople mint).
Fig. 6. Solidus of Justinian I.
Fig. 7. 20 nummia piece of Justin II struck at Cyzicus mint. The figure seated
          to the left on the obverse is the emperor, the figure to the right is
          the empress Sophia.

TIBERIUS II (578-582 A.D. — the first Tiberius being the long forgotten successor to the first Roman emperor Augustus) who in spite of his unique election was a fairly good emperor. Tiberius married his daughter to one of his generals

MAURICE TIBERIUS (582-602 A.D.) who succeeded Tiberius II. Maurice was an industrious emperor and a fairly good soldier. Things were favorable for a while, but several bad decisions by Maurice in military matters created an insurrection among the Balkan troops and Maurice and his entire family were brutally murdered by the leader of the mutiny

PHOCAS (602-610 A.D.) who then crowned himself emperor. Phocas met with military disaster from both the east and the west, while at home he launched a campaign of terror and murder to keep himself in power. Finally, the Exarch of the province of Africa, Heraclius, who had been kept in office only because of his personal popularity with his people, was persuaded to launch a campaign to relieve the nation. The Exarch sent his son, also called Heraclius, to Constantinople with a strong fleet. When he arrived, Phocas was seized and executed, and the younger Heraclius was proclaimed emperor, initiating the Heraclian period.

SUMMARY OF THE COINAGE OF THE JUSTINIANEAN PERIOD

The bust of the emperor, diademed or helmeted, is now found facing on the major coins although a side portrait is occasionally found, usually on the minor coins. In the obverse legend, the emperor is still hailed as D(ominus) N(ostrum), P(ius), F(elix), AVG(ustus) but the old titles are changing. Leo I in the Theodosian Period called himself PP

9

REPRESENTATIVE OBVERSE LEGENDS OF THE JUSTINIANEAN PERIOD

Anastasius I, 491-518
1. DN ANASTASIVS PF AVG
Justin I, 518-527
1. DN IVSTINVS PF AVG
Justin I and Justinian I, 527
1. DN IVSTIN CT IVSTINIAN PP AVG
Justinian I, 527-565
1. DN IVSTINIANVS PP AVG
Justin II, 565-578
1. DN IVSTINVS PF (PIVS, IVN) AVG
Tiberius II, 578-582
1. Эm TIb CONSTANT PP AVI
2. Эm CONSTANTINVS PP AG
Maurice Tiberius, 582-602
1. DN MAVRC TIb PP AVG
2. DN MAVRICIVS PF AVG
Focas
1. DN (DM) FOCAS PERP AVG 2. DN FOCA P AVG

Representative Reverse Legends
Common to all reigns:
    1. GLORIA ROMANORVM
    2. VICTORIA AVGGG (AVGVSTORVM)
  (Denominational reverses in silver)
    3. CN (250 mummia)
    4. PKE (125 mummia)
    5. PK (120 mummia)
  (Denominational reverses in bronze)

6. M or XXXX (40 mummia)	10. IS (16 mummia)	
7. K or XX (20 mummia)	11. IB (12 mummia)	
8. I or X (10 mummia)	12. H (8 mummia)	
9. E or C (5 mummia)	13. S (6 mummia)	

Legends restricted to certain reigns:
Tiberius II
  1. VICTORIA TIbERI RTVIH 2. XXX (30 mummia)
  3. ϤICTOR TIbERI AϤϤ
Focas
  1. VICTORI FOCAS AVϤ   2. ϕK

or PERPET (perpetuus) AVG(ustus) and this legend was used by many later rulers. Later in the Iconoclastic Period Leo III introduced the term P(erpetuo) A(ugustus) MVL (ta) followed in the Amorian era with the Greek titles of Despot and Autocrat. The use of the Greek title for king, "Basileus," was introduced in the Heraclian period supplanting the DN and AVG of the earlier years.

On the reverse, the personification of Victory is still encountered in the Justinianean period and an occasional reverse will still show the emperor in a warlike attitude. The christogram and the cross are more frequently encountered in this period, especially on gold and silver coins. Imperial monograms are common. The reforms of Anastasius altered the reverses of the bronze coinage as previously noted. Coins are now commonly dated in the bronze series usually with the word ANNO to the left of the denominational symbol and the regal year to the right. The mint mark is still found in the exergual space on the reverse. The emperor Zeno changed the name of Antioch to Theopolis for a time and the mint mark was changed accordingly, persisting into this period.

HISTORICAL OUTLINE — HERACLIAN PERIOD

HERACLIUS (610-641 A.D.), after his elevation to the throne, was beset with the sins of his predecessor in the forms of Balkan and Eastern wars. However, in the face of great hardship, he was finally able to completely crush the Persians, who had even besieged his capital in the earlier part of his reign. The campaigns of Heraclius in Persia are one of the most brilliant chapters in the entire Byzantine drama. Early in his rule, Heraclius associated his eldest son

HERACLIUS CONSTANTINE as co-emperor. Later another son by his second marriage,

HERACLEONAS was also associated in the government. When the aged Heraclius died, 641, having the bitter knowledge that all of his Persian conquests were being undone by the upsurging Arabs inspired by Mohammad, both sons were given a taste of rule. Heraclius Constantine died very shortly after his succession, leaving Heracleonas as sole emperor. Heraclius Constantine however, had left a son

CONSTANTINE III* (641-668 A.D.) who was elected emperor after a popular revolt overthrew his uncle. Constantine III was a harsh but efficient ruler who successfully defended his empire against its enemies. He was murdered by a bath attendant in Syracuse and was succeeded by his son

CONSTANTINE IV (668-685 A.D.) who was left to face a great siege of Constantinople by the Arabs. His defense was brilliant and he actually forced the Arabs on the defensive. Unfortunately, Constantine IV died quite young and his hard headed son succeeded as

JUSTINIAN II (685-695 A.D., 1st Reign) and promptly started another Arab war. This time the empire met with many reverses in the field,

---

* Constantines I and II were considered to have been Constantine the Great, the founder of Constantinople, and his son Constantine who ruled briefly in Gaul after his father's death.

while at home Justinian governed in a harsh and stupid manner eventually inciting revolt led by a general

LEONTIUS (695-698 A.D.) who was in turn overthrown by a naval revolt led by

TIBERIUS III (698-705 A.D.). In the meanwhile, Justinian who had been exiled to the city of Cherson escaped captivity and aided by the Bulgarians returned to Constantinople and deposed Tiberius III, then

JUSTINIAN II (705-711 A.D., 2nd reign) proceeded to remove all of those who had aided in his first overthrow. Leontius and Tiberius were both murdered and a major blood bath was initiated. Justinian decided to destroy Cherson, his place of exile, but the troops sent to perform the destruction, rebelled and returned home to overthrow Justinian for the second time. After his execution, a general

FILEPICUS BARDANES (711-713 A.D.) became ruler but a series of reverses led to the election as emperor of

ANASTASIUS II (713-716), a civilian, who had been a counselor of Filepicus. The elevation of a civilian did not sit well with the military element, and when Anastasius attempted to reform the troops, the army revolted, electing an inoffensive tax official

THEODOSIUS III (716-717 A.D.) to the throne. Theodosius was a sincere, likable person but not of imperial stature. He tried to do a good job but the threat of a major Arab invasion, coupled with provincial civil war, led the general of the Anatolic theme (administrative district) to seize power as Leo III. As a rare change from the usual, Leo did not execute his predecessor but allowed him to quietly retire into the country where he lived for many years after his deposition.

Fig. 8.   Semissis of Heraclius.
Fig. 9.   Solidus of Heraclius and Heraclius Constantine. The bust of Heraclius is to the left and that of his son is to the right.
Fig. 10.   Hexagram of Heraclius and Heraclius Constantine.
Fig. 11.   Solidus of Justinian II (1st reign).

SUMMARY OF THE COINAGE OF THE HERACLIAN PERIOD

The coinage of the East Roman Empire is by now acquiring the characteristics that give it the characteristic "Byzantine" appearance with which the average collector is generally somewhat acquainted. The busts on the obverse are facing except on a few minor coins where the traditional bust right is still retained. On gold and silver coins, the cross and VICTORIA AVGG legend has almost entirely supplanted all other forms. The bronze coins still retain the denomination types introduced by Anastasius. The Greek style of lettering is more obvious, especially after the reign of Justinian II. Justinian II also introduced a reverse of the bust of Christ and the obverse SER CHRISTI legend, a type which was not repeated until after the great iconoclastic controversy. Although the cross and christogram had been used for centuries, this is the first actual instance of the portrayal of Christ on a Byzantine coin.

The coinage of this period is noted for its wretched workmanship, especially those pieces struck by the provincial mints. Often the sequence of imperial titles is so jumbled and the lettering done so poorly that it is impossible to make out an intelligible legend. The figures are quite grotesque at times, bearing little real resemblance to the human form, while the facial appearance of the busts is masklike. Mint marks are still found in the exergual space on most coins but many of the smaller mints have disappeared as the barbarians have reconquered the western territories regained by Justinian I while the Arabs have over-run Africa.

Some mention should be made of graffiti, or scratched inscriptions, which are found on many coins of this era. These take the form of minute scratched symbols on any smooth surface on either reverse or obverse and usually take the form of Greek letters or geometrical designs. It is believed that they are probably some sort of banker or merchant marks similar to the well known "chop marks" of the modern orient. An excellent discussion of these markings is found in an article by Holzer in the *Numismatic Review* of July, 1944. It is sufficient here to bring them to the readers' attention. Graffiti are not restricted only to this period but are found throughout most of the Byzantine era up to the fall of Constantinople during the Fourth Crusade. They are least common during the eighth to tenth centuries, while fairly prevalent during the fourth to seventh centuries and then again in the eleventh and twelfth centuries.

Also, in many history texts, the emperor Constantine III is often called Constans II. Just exactly why this discrepancy exists is not completely understood since he always referred to himself as Constantine in the official papers of the time and on his coinage. In this paper, we have followed Goodacre and referred to him in the tables by his real name disregarding the term Constans II. His father, Heraclius Constantine (who is said to be the true Constantine III by those who call his son Constans), did not live long enough to strike coinage in his own name. However on the coins struck with his father he always used his full name and if he had struck his own coinage, he probably would have called himself simply "Heraclius" or retained the full "Heraclius Constantine" thus completely differentiating himself from his son. The name Constans is confusing and in my opinion should not be used in reference to Constantine III especially in numismatics where the legends on his coins, when complete, clearly read "Constantine."

REPRESENTATIVE OBVERSE LEGENDS OF THE HERACLIAN PERIOD

Heraclius, 610-641
1. DN HERACLIVS PP AVG
2. DN ЄRACΛIO PP AV
Heraclius with Heraclius Constantine
1. DD NN HERACLIVS ET HERA CONST PP AV
Constantine III, 641-668
1. DN CONSTANTINVS PP AVG   2. IҍPЄR COҊST
Constantine III with Constantine IV
1. ϽN CONSƮANƬINЧS C CONSƮAN
Constantine IV, 668-685
1. ϽN CONSƮANƬINЧS
Justinian II, 685-695 (1st reign)
1. D IЧSJINIANЧS PЄ AV
2. D IЧSJINIANЧS SЄR CHRISJI
Tiberius III, 698-705
1. D ƮIbЄRIЧS PЄ AV
Justinian II, 705-711 (2nd reign) with son Tiberius
1. DN IЧSTINIANЧS ЄT TIbЄRIЧS PP A
Filepicus, 711-713
1. DN FILЄPICЧS MЧLTЧS AN
Anastasius II, 713-716
1. ϽN ARTЄMIЧS ANASTASIЧS MЧL
Theodosius III, 716-717
1. ϽN ƮЄOϽOSIЧS MЧLA

REPRESENTATIVE REVERSE LEGENDS

1. VICTORIA AVҪҪ
2. ϽЄЧS AϽIЧJA ROMANIS (God help the Romans)
3. IhS CRISƮOS RЄX RЄJNANJIЧM (Jesus Christ, King of
   Kings. Present after Justinian's 1st reign)
4. ЄN TʋTO NIKA (In this we conquer)
5. RM (Abbreviation for Roman)
      Denominational reverses in bronze
6. M (40 nummia)   8. I (10 nummia)
7. K or XX (20 nummia)   9. Є (5 nummia)

HISTORICAL OUTLINE OF THE ISAURIAN-AMORIAN OR ICONOCLASTIC PERIOD

LEO III (717-741 A.D.) was able to withstand the Arab siege of his capital and broke the most concerted attempt on the Christian east ever undertaken by the Arabs. Once peace had returned to the empire, Leo proceeded to attack the use of images in worship as a form of idolatry and ordered their destruction starting the great Iconoclastic controversy which lasted for over one hundred years. Leo was succeeded by his strong and efficient son

CONSTANTINE V (741-775 A.D.) who continued his policies. Constantine was not popular with the people who generally supported the iconodules or image supporters. Constantine was followed by his physically weak but intelligent and strong willed son

LEO IV (775-780 A.D.) who ruled intelligently until his death when his young son

CONSTANTINE VI (780-797 A.D.) became emperor under the regency of his beautiful mother, IRENE. Irene and her son ruled jointly until he attained his majority. At that time Irene was anxious to keep her power, and although the army initially forced her into a minor role, she was able by 797 to overthrow, imprison, and blind her son.

IRENE (797-802 A.D.) then seized sole power. In spite of her brutal deed, she managed to maintain herself as empress for five years before she was overthrown and eventually executed, by starvation according to some sources, by

NICEPHORUS I (802-811 A.D.) who became emperor. During Irene's reign, the Pope availed himself of the opportunity of female rule to proclaim the establishment of a new Roman Empire and crown Charles, King of the Franks, as emperor. Nicephorus ruled well until he fell fighting the Bulgarians and was succeeded by his son

STAURACIUS (811 A.D.) who unfortunately was also mortally wounded in the same battle. After a short time, Stauracius died after being forced to create his brother-in-law

MICHAEL I (811-813 A.D.) emperor. Michael also was defeated in battle by the Bulgarians, probably through treachery by his trusted general Leo, who then instigated a revolt and had himself crowned as

LEO V (813-820 A.D.). Leo ruled fairly well but in the course of a plot, instigated by the friends of an old military companion he had imprisoned, was murdered at the altar while he celebrated Christmas Mass. The former colleague, an Amorian, was then crowned

MICHAEL II (820-828 A.D.) starting the Amorian dynasty. Michael ruled fairly well according to the times and at his death was followed by his educated son

THEOPHILUS (829-842 A.D.). Theophilus was an ardent iconoclast, one of the last, but otherwise ruled fairly well. He was very fond of show and was famous for his golden throne with golden lions that roared and golden birds which would sing. Theophilus prided himself on his fairness and would hold courts where any and all could ask for justice. This didn't prevent him from roasting several iconodules alive however. At his death, Theophilus left his minor son

MICHAEL III (842-867 A.D.) under the regency of his mother, Theodora. Theodora in her effort to keep power encouraged her son to all forms of excess in which he cooperated so fully that he was known to his people

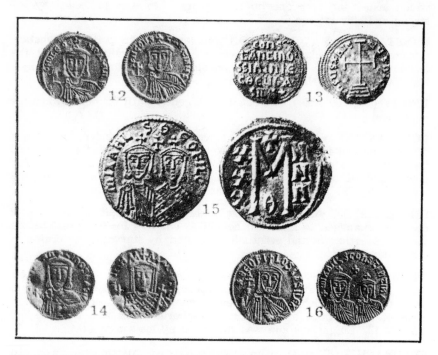

Fig. 12.   **Solidus of Leo III with his son, Constantine V, depicted on the reverse.**

Fig. 13.   **Miliaresion of Constantine VI and Irene.**

Fig. 14.   **Solidus of Constantine VI with Irene depicted on the reverse.**

Fig. 15.   **Large bronze piece of Michael II and his son Theophilus. (A.N.S. Collection).**

Fig. 16.   **Solidus of Theophilus. His father Michael II (on left) and his eldest son Constantine (on right) are depicted on the reverse.**

as "the Drunkard." Nevertheless, Michael assumed the throne. He was very fond of riding and the skill of one of his grooms, a youth from Macedonia, Basil by name, impressed Michael so much that he made Basil co-emperor. Later when it appeared that Michael intended to depose him, Basil took the preferred method of the period and had his benefactor murdered in bed. Basil then ruled alone as BASIL I.

During the reign of Constantine V, an usurper ARTAVASDUS was able to seize the throne for a short time. He issued a few coins which are extremely rare today. His obverse legend is included in the tables mostly for the sake of completeness.

Leo III, 717-741
    1. D LEON PE AV   2. ⊖NO LEON PA M4L
Constantine V, 741-775
    1. GN CONSZANZINYS   COn
Constantine V with son Leo IV   SZAnZI
    1. CONSZANZInOS S LEOn O nEOS   2.   nESLEON
Artavasdus, 742-744 (usurper)   ECⵙⵙYbA
    1. G ARZA4ASDOS M4L   SILIS
Leo IV, 775-780 with son Constantine VI
    1. LEON VSSESON COnSZAnZInOS O NEOS
    2.   LEOn
         SCOnSZ
         AnZInEE
         CⵙE4bA
         SILIS   COnS
Constantine VI and Irene, 780-797   ZAnIno
    1. COnSZAnZInOS S IR   2.   SSIRInI
Irene, 797-802   ECⵙEYbA
    1. EIRINH bASILISSH   SILIS
    2. EIPInH bAS
Nicephorus I, 802-811
    1. NICIFORS bASIL   2. nICIFOR bAS'
Michael I, 811-813
    1. MIXAHL bA   MIXA
Michael I with son Theophylactus   HLSⵙEOFV
    1. MIXAHL S ⵙEOF'   2.   LACZ.EEC
Leo V, 813-820   bASILISRO
    1. LEON bASILE '   MAIOn
Leo V with son Constantine   ⚊LEOn
    1. LEON S COnSZA´   2. SCOnStAn
                           tInEECEE4
Michael II, 820-829   bASILISRO
    1. MIXAHL bASILE   MAIOn
    2. MXA
Michael II with son Theophilus   ⚊MIXA
    1. MIXAHL S ⵙEOFILOS   2. HLSⵙEOFI
Theophilus, 829-842   LEECEE4
    1. ⵙEOFILOS bASILS   bASIBISRO
    2.   ⚊EEOFI   MAIOn
       LOSⵙ4LOS   with son Constantine
       XRISt4SPIS   1. ⵙEOFILOS S COnStAnt'
       tOSEnAVtO
       bASILE4RO
       MAIOn

Theophilus with son Michael III   ☧ ꝋꝋꝋ
after the death of son Constant-   FILOSSMI
ine.   1.   XAHLꝎꝎ
                                     bASILIRO

Theodora, regent for Michael III   MAIOn
   1. ☧ ꝋꝎ0ORA ꝺꝎSPVnA
Theodora with Michael III and his   ☧ MIXA
sister Thecla   1.   HLꝋꝎ0ORA
                                     SꝋꝎCL.AꝎCꝋ'
Michael III, 842-867   bASILISRO
   1. MIXAHL bASILꝎ   AIOn
   2. MIXAHL b   3. ☧MIXA
   3. ☧MIhAꝎL IMPERAT   PISTOSbA
                                 SILꝎꝐSRO
                                 MAIOn

REPRESENTATIVE REVERSE LEGENDS

Common to all reigns:
  1. VICTORIA AVꝘ   4. M (40 nummia)
  2. IVCTORIA AVꝘTO   5. K (20 nummia)
  3. IhSꝐS XRIStꝐS nICA   6. I (10 nummia)
Restricted to certain reigns:
  Constantine V
1.   LꝎON PA MꝐL (Bust facing, if bearded, Leo III;
if beardless, Leo IV)
  Leo IV
1. LꝎO PAP'COnSt AntOC PAtHR (Busts of Leo III to
the left and Constantine V to the right)
  Constantine VI
1. HRHnI AVGꝐtR (Facing bust of Irene)
  Nicephorus I
1. STAꝐRACI   (both have facing bust of
2. StAVRACIS ꝺꝎSPOS   Stauracius)
  Michael I
1. ꝋꝎOFVLACtOS ꝺꝎSPOS   (both have facing bust of
2. ꝋꝎꝼOV   Theophylactus)
  Theophilus
1. CVRIE bOHꝋH tO SO ꝺOVLO ☧ (Cross on two steps)
2. ☧MIXAHL S COnStAntInS (Facing busts of Michael
II and son Constantine)
3. MIXAHL (Facing bust of son Michael III)
  Michael III
1. bACIΛꝎIOC   (Facing busts of co-emperor
2. ☧bASILIꝐS RꝎX ☧   Basil I)

SUMMARY OF THE COINAGE OF THE ISAURIAN-AMORIAN OR INCONOCLASTIC PERIOD

The obverse busts, and the reverse bust which became very common in this period, are noted for their stiffness of execution. It is almost impossible to differentiate one emperor from another, or even from an empress, by facial expressions alone due to the formal pictorialization popular during this era. The practice of placing imperial busts on both sides of the coins arose from the iconoclastic controversy over iconds and was adopted apparently as a polite way of removing religious symbols from the coinage. The usual method of placing the busts was to show the ruling emperor on the obverse, either alone or with some member of his family, and the sons or heir apparent on the reverse. The empress Irene during her reign had her bust on both sides of her coins. A very nice example of this sort of thing is shown in the obverse legends and reverse busts in the earlier part of this period. Leo III initially struck coins similar to his predecessors, but when he opened the iconoclastic controversy, he removed the traditional reverse types from the coins and replaced them with his son's bust. When Constantine V succeeded to the throne, he continued his father's policies and used both his father's and his son's busts as reverse types, referring to the former as "PAP" or grandfather and the latter as "O NEOS" or the younger. Leo, following the same principles, called himself "VSSESON" which Mattingly suggests means "the son and the less," undoubtedly referring to his relationship to his father Constantine V whom he sometimes referred to as "PATHR" (the father) on his coins. Constantine VI, the son of Leo IV, is called "O NEOS" on his father's coins.

The emperor Stauracius is found only on his father's reverses where he is titled "DESPOT" in contrast to the more imposing title of BASIL (king) used by Nicephorus on the obverse. The last use of the old Roman title "IMPERATOR" is on a coin of Michael III.

The miliaresion was first struck by Constantine V in this period and persists as the standard silver coin for several hundred years. Characteristically, the miliaresion had an inscription type obverse and a cross reverse with a "King of Kings" or similar legend. Inscriptions on the miliaresion are usually five or six lines long and contain the imperial name or names (as many as four people are named on some of these coins) and titles. On the first issue the words "EC ΘEV bASILIS" (To God Emperor) are used while later the word "PISTOS" (faithful) is added in the sequence. After the reign of Michael I and Theophylactus the word "ROMAION" (of the Romans) is commonly found after the title "BASILEVS" to point out that Byzantium considered itself as the true Roman Empire in contrast to the recently established Empire of Charles of the Franks. The cross before the emperor's name is first used by Leo V and helps differentiate his coinage from that of earlier Leos.

The old denominational symbols are still found on the bronze coins but toward the end of the Iconoclastic period tend to be replaced with inscription type reverses similar to those found on the silver. The symbol "M" persists longer than the others but by the advent of the Macedonian period even this symbol has been largely replaced by inscriptions, monograms, and abbreviations of the imperial names.

Greek letter forms are common during this era and are used interchangeably with Latin forms. Stylized letters are also frequently encountered, especially forms of omega, "V," and "G."

HISTORICAL OUTLINE OF THE MACEDONIAN PERIOD

BASIL I (867-886 A.D.) in spite of his colorful method of attaining the throne turned out to be a good emperor. He kept the empire intact both physically and economically. After his death, he was followed by his very learned son

LEO VI (886-912 A.D.) who attained quite a reputation for his academic works. The empire remained healthy during his reign and with a few exceptions was militarily quiet. At his death, he was succeeded by his brother

ALEXANDER (886-913 A.D.) who had been nominally his co-emperor for years. Alexander had been content to remain in the background and enjoy high living. After his brother's death, Alexander turned to government and was fairly good considering his lack of practice. When Alexander died shortly afterwards, Leo's son

CONSTANTINE VII (912-959 A.D.) became emperor. Like his father, Constantine was intellectually inclined and left the actual rule to a series of co-emperors, the first of which was his father-in-law, a competent admiral named

ROMANUS I (919-944 A.D.) who ruled well during his many years as co-emperor. Toward the end of his reign, his own sons decided that they would seize power and remove both their father and Constantine from power. The people sided with Constantine, however, and the revolt failed. After the death of Romanus, Constantine ruled in his own name until his death when his son

ROMANUS II (959-963 A.D.) became emperor. Romanus II died shortly after his accession and his infant sons, Basil and Constantine, were crowned with their extremely attractive mother Theophano as regent.

BASIL II (assumed throne 963, actual rule 976-1025 A.D.), the eldest son, was a hard willed, tough soldier, who led the empire to its greatest military heights when he attained his majority. He drove the Bulgarians back to the empire's boundaries earning for himself the title of "Slayer of Bulgarians." He patterned himself on his first guardian Nicephorus I and led the strict life of a monk during the latter part of his reign.

CONSTANTINE VIII (assumed throne 963, actual rule 1025-1028 A.D.), the younger brother, was a mild individual and his role reign after his brother's death was somewhat inept. Before continuing, the two guardians that were co-emperors during the minority of Constantine and his brother Basil should be considered. The first of these was the greatest soldier of the age, the man who destroyed the pirates of Crete and who drove the Mohammedans back from the boundaries of the empire.

NICEPHORUS II (963-969 A.D.) Phocas. After her husband died, Theophano was attracted to Nicephorus and managed to arrange for her marriage to the general. Nicephorus was an excellent ruler, strictly respecting the rights of his wards. His reign was, as his life had been, a series of successful military campaigns. However, he excited the suspicions of his relative

JOHN I (969-976 A.D.). Zimisces who instigated his murder, with, some believe, the aid of Theophano. John was as good a soldier as his uncle and is famed for his brilliant defeats of the Russians. John died suddenly from fever, some say poison, in 976 A.D. and, as noted previously, Basil became the senior emperor with his brother taking the lesser role. After Basil died, Constantine ruled alone, and the succession was again in doubt since Constantine had only two daughters, Zoe and Theodora. When it appeared his end was in sight, Constantine had Zoe marry an obscure noble named

Fig. 17.　Large bronze piece of Leo VI.
Fig. 18.　Large bronze coin of Constantine VII struck during the regency of his mother Zoe. Constantine is the smaller figure to the left and Zoe is the larger figure to the right.
Fig. 19.　Miliaresion of Nicephorus II.
Fig. 20.　Solidus of Basil II and Constantine VIII. Basil, as senior emperor, is shown to the left while the younger Constantine is to the right of the obverse face.
Fig. 21.　Anonymous bronze coin of the late 10th century (A.N.S. Collection)
Fig. 22.　Solidus of Constantine IX.

ROMANUS III (1028-1034 A.D.) who had been forced to divorce his original wife. Romanus died in the bath (some say murdered) after a few years, and Zoe married a Paphalagonian, who ascended the throne as

MICHAEL IV (1034-1041 A.D.). Michael, however handsome, turned out to be a hopeless epileptic but in spite of his handicap tried hard to be a good ruler. He fought battles literally tied to his saddle and gave a good account of himself considering his physical state. On his death, Zoe adopted her husband's nephew,

MICHAEL V (1041-1042) and had him created emperor. Michael was a thankless person and tried to remove Zoe and her sister from the scene. The people of Constantinople rose in revolt and Michael was deposed, blinded and imprisoned by the two sisters

ZOE and **THEODORA** (1042 A.D.) who ruled jointly for several months as sole rulers. Zoe, however, married an old suitor

CONSTANTINE IX (1042-1054 A.D.) who became emperor. Constantine ruled until his death (Zoe dying in 1050 A.D.), and was succeeded by

THEODORA (1054-1056) who ruled alone for about two years. When she was dying, she created an elderly general

MICHAEL VI (1056-1057 A.D.) emperor. Michael had been a good soldier in the past but he was unfit to assume the throne of a now somewhat shaky nation. A series of insurrections developed and a representative of the great feudal aristocracy of Byzantium, Isaac Comnenus, was elected emperor, ending the Macedonian dynasty.

SUMMMARY OF THE COINAGE OF THE MACEDONIAN PERIOD

The facing bust on the obverse is now the accepted form and Greek titles and letter forms are standard. Busts are still found on reverses as in the iconoclastic era, but the reappearance of religious forms on the reverse denotes the final defeat of that group. The "King of Kings" and "Christ Conquers" legends herald the advent of a period of ecclesiastical reverse types that persist until the final collapse of the empire in 1453. Inscriptions are still common obverse and reverse types, especially on silver and bronze coins. The titles used in these legends are similar to those used by the iconoclasts with a few exceptions. The abbreviation "EN X.W" (EN EXPICTW or "in Christ") replaces the "EC ΘEV" of the earlier period while Leo VI introduced "EVCEbH" (Eusebes or Pious) into his legends. The term "Basileus Romaion" is frequently abbreviated to "b R." Constantine VII introduced the title "AVTOKRA-TOR" to the imperial titles and also called himself "porphyrogenitus" or "born in the purple" (ΠOPFVROG'). Occasionally during this period, a bust will appear on the side opposite the inscription on the miliaresion, but unless the imperial names are clearly mentioned (not abbreviations) with the bust, we still consider that side the reverse. If a cross and legends are opposite the inscription, the inscription is always considered the obverse. This too is the era of numerous co-emperors and frequently three or even four names will be found in legends since the emperors commonly struck coins with their own bust on the obverse and their colleagues either named or depicted on the reverse. The anonymous bronze series starts during the reign of John I in this period (see introduction

REPRESENTATIVE OBVERSE LEGENDS OF THE MACEDONIAN PERIOD

Basil, 867-886
1. ǂbASILIOS bASILЄVS

with son Constantine
1. ǂbASI
LIOS CЄ
COnSƬAn
ƬIn'PISZV
bASILIS
ROMЄO

Basil with sons Constantine and Leo
1. ǂLЄOn bASIL' COnSƬ' AYΓΓ

Leo VI, 886-912
1. LЄON ЄN XW bASILЄVS ROMWN
2. LЄON bASILЄVS ROM X
3. LЄWn
CnX.WЄV
SЄbHSbASI
LЄVSRW
AIWn
4. ΛЄ

Leo with son Constantine VII
1. LЄOn ЄT COnSJAnJ' AYΓΓ'ROM'
2. ǂLЄOnCЄ
COnSTANTI
n'ЄNX:WЄV
SЄbISbASI
LI'ROM

Leo VI and Alexander
1. ǂLЄON S ALЄΞAnΓROS
2. ǂLЄOn S ALЄΞA
3. ΛA

Alexander, 912-913
1. ALЄXAndROS AYΓΓ SƬOS ROM
2. A

Constantine VII, 913-959
1. ǂCONSƬAnƬ' AVƬCRAƬOR'
2. COnST' bASIL' ROM'

with mother Zoe
1. ǂCONSƬAnƬ'CЄ ZOH'b'

Constantine VII with son Romanus II
1. ǂCONSƬ'Ƭ'CЄ ROMAn'b'ROM
2. COnSƬAnƬ CЄ ROMAn AYΓΓ b'R'
3. ǂCONST'Ƭ'
ΠORFVROΓ'
CЄROMAnO'
ЄnXWЄVSЄb'
bRWMЄOn

Constantine VII with Romanus I
1. ǂCOnSƬAnƬInOS CЄ ROMAn ЄN XW bR
2. CONSƬAnƬ CЄ ROMAn AYΓ b R

Romanus I, 919-944
1. ROMAnO ЄN ΘX b'R'
2. ǂRWMAn bASILIЄVS RWM

with Constantine VII
1. ǂROMAn'ЄT COnSƬAnƬ'AVΓΓ b

Romanus with son Christopher
1. ROMAn ЄT XPISƬOFO' AYΓΓ b'

Nicephorus II, 963-969
1. ǂnICIFR bASIL ROM
2. ǂΘЄOTOC'b'HΘ'nICHF'ΘЄSP
3. ǂnICHF'
CnX'WΛVƬO
CRΛT'ЄVSЄb'
bΛSILЄVS
RWMΛIW'

Nicephorus II and Basil II
1. NIKHǂOP' KAI BACIΛ AVƬ'RP

REPRESENTATIVE OBVERSE LEGENDS OF
THE MACEDONIAN PERIOD

John I, 969-976   IWΛnn'
  1. ŦΘΕΟΤΟC bOHΘ IW ƏΕSP   2.   ΕnX. WΛVϤΟ
                                     CRΛT, ΕVSb
Basil II and Constantine VIII,   bΛSILΕVS
    976- 1025   RWMΛIW'
1. ŦbΛSIL'
CCWnSϤΛb'
ΠORF. VROϛ'   2. ŦbΛSIL C COnSϤANTI b R
ΠISϤOIbΛS
  RWMΛIW

Constantine VIII alone, 1025-1028
    CWnSϤAnϤIn' BASILΕYS ROM
Romanus III, 1028-1034
    ΘCΕ BOHΘ' RWMAnW
Michael IV, 1034-1041
    ŦMIXΛHL bΛSILΕYS RM
Michael V, 1041-1042
    ŦMIXAHL AϞTOCRAT
Constantine IX, 1042-1055   ΘKΕR. Θ
  1. ŦCWnSϤAnnOS bASILΕVS RM   3.   KWNCTAN
  2. ŦCWnSϤAnϤn bASILΕVS RM   TINWΔΕC
                                     ΠOTH TW
Theodora, 1055-1056   MONOMA
    ŦΘΕΟΔWR AΛΓOVCT
Michael VI, 1056-1057
  1. ŦMIXAHL AVtOCRAt
  2. ŦMIXAHL ΔΕCΠOT

                REPRESENTATIVE REVERSE LEGENDS
Common to all reigns
1. ŦIhS XPS RΕX RΕϛNANTϞM Ŧ (Jesus Christ, King of Kings)
2. IhSϞS XPIStϞS nICA   (Jesus Christ Conquers)

Reverse legends restricted to certain reigns
Basil I   Basil I with son Constantine
    ŦbΛSIL   ŦbΛSIL
   IOSΕnΘΕO   SCOnStAn
   bASILΕVS   tInOSΕnΘŌ
   ROMΕOn·   bASILΕISR
                            OMAOn

Basil I with son Constantine and Leo

  ✠bASIL
  COnStAn
  tSLEOnЄn
  ΘObASILS
  ROMЄON

Leo VI alone   Leo VI and Alexander
 LEON   LEON
ЄnΘЄObA   SALЄⰗAn
SILЄVSR 1. GROSbASIL 2. ΛЄ
 OMЄON   ROMЄOn

Constantine VII with Zoe   Romanus I
  ✠COnS   ✠RWMA
  tAntInO   n'ЄnΘЄWbA
  CCZOHbA   SILЄVSRW
  SILISRO   MAIWn
  MЄOn

Constantine VII with Romanus I
  ✠COnS   ✠COnST'
  tAntIn   ЄnΘЄObA
  ЄnΘObAS   SILЄVSR
  IL'ROM   OMЄOn

Romanus I with Constantine VII and his own sons
 Stefan and Constantine
   ✠ROMАⱤO   Nicephorus II
   COhStАnt.   ✠NICHF'
   STЄFAnOS   ЄnΘЄWbA
   CЄCOnSTA'   SILЄVSRW
   ЄNX'Wb'R'   MAIWn

John I
 IhSΥS XRIStΥS nICΑ* (around edge of coin) with IWΑN
(around center medallion with bust of John)

Basil II and Constantine VIII
 ЄN tOVtW nICΑ bASIL ЄI C CWnSt (with busts of
both emperors between standard)

Constantine IX
 H RΛΛXЄPNITICA (Virgin orans) with $\overline{MP}$ $\overline{\Theta V}$
in field.

and appendix) and the time honoured denominational symbols of Anastasius disappear from the bronze coinage. Abbreviations of Christ's name and that of the Virgin (IC XC and MP OV) appear during the Macedonia period but do not reach the prominence they later attain as reverse legends.

HISTORICAL OUTLINE OF THE COMNENIAN PERIOD

ISAAC I (1057-1059 A.D.) Comnenus, unable to solve the increasingly difficult problems of the empire, retired in frustration to private life and nominated his colleague as emperor

CONSTANTINE X (1059-1067 A.D.) of the House of Ducas. Constantine battled with little success against the problems of decline enhanced by the encroachments of the Turks in the east and the Normans in the west. When he died, his widow married one of the more dashing generals of the period

ROMANUS IV (1067-1071 A.D.) who ruled with EUDOCIA Makrembolitissa as regents for her sons. Romanus tried hard to push back the Turks and had some success. However, when he was trapped and captured at the disastrous battle of Manzikert in 1071 A.D., he was deposed in a palace revolution. The defeat at Manzikert opened Asia Minor to Turkish conquest and they soon were overrunning the countryside. Eudocia's eldest son

MICHAEL VII (1071-1078 A.D.) was crowned ruler. Michael was a weak, unpopular man who was soon overthrown by

NICEPHORUS III (1078-1081 A.D.) Botaniates whose reign was a continual series of insurrections. Finally a man of credit and intelligence, Alexius Comnenus was able to establish himself as

ALEXIUS I (1081-1118 A.D.). Alexius was an extremely clever man and managed by scheming and fighting to regain some of the stability the empire had lost under his predecessors. The First Crusade took place during his reign and through this event Alexius was able to regain the territory in Asia Minor that the Turks had seized. He also tried to reform his corrupt government with some success. At his death, he was followed by his son

JOHN II (1118-1143 A.D.). John was an extremely popular ruler and possessed one of the finest characters of any of the long line of Byzantine emperors. He consolidated his father's gains and the empire actually had a period of some prosperity. When he died, however, he was succeeded by his extremely colorful son

MANUEL I (1143-1180 A.D.), a knight-errant in the best story book fashion. Manuel spent most of his reign dashing from one battlefield to another with more or less success. Unfortunately, although usually winning, he always seemed to be fighting the wrong war and to complete his folly, he lost the one battle in Asia Minor he should have won, Myriokephalon. The Second Crusade took place in his reign but Manuel received little profit from the expedition. It has to be admitted that Manuel was a dashing figure, afraid of nothing, but unfortunately, the empire needed a real diplomat like his grandfather rather than a military hero. When Manuel died, his young son

ALEXIUS II (1180-1183 A.D.) became emperor. However, a nephew of John II, Andronicus Comnenus, who was equally as colorful as Manuel but in a slightly more seamy way having seen the inside of just about every jail in Byzantium, managed to become a regent. Andronicus then removed his young ward in the best Byzantine fashion and ruled as

ANDRONICUS I (1183-1185 A.D.). Andronicus started out with good ideas but his reform movement ran into opposition and the usual blood bath developed. An inoffensive noble, Isaac Angelus, was brought under suspicion and in self defense he murdered one of the emperor's agents starting a revolt ending with the crowning of himself as

ISAAC II (1185-1195 A.D.). Isaac was a harmless soul who spent most of his time worrying about ikons. The Third Crusade occurred during his reign but Isaac was not capable of turning their victories to his benefit. A revolt finally placed his brother

ALEXIUS III (1195-1203 A.D.) on the throne and Isaac was imprisoned and blinded. Alexius was a weak ruler interested only in the pleasures of the table. The son of Isaac,

ALEXIUS IV (1203-1204 A.D.) managed to interest the members of the Fourth Crusade to reinstate him and his father as rulers. The crusaders went to Constantinople and deposed Alexius III, replacing the aged Isaac II and his son on the throne. Unfortunately, the restored rulers were unable to pay the price agreed upon for these services and the Crusaders stormed the city. An emergency session deposed the Angeli and placed

ALEXIUS V (1204 A.D.) on the throne. However, he was unable to hold the capital and the crusaders took the city and sacked it from top to bottom. Alexius was later captured and murdered. The crusaders then divided up the empire, theoretically to a great extent, and the Byzantine empire was forced into exile, ending the Comnenian period.

SUMMARY OF THE COINAGE OF THE COMNENIAN PERIOD

Ecclesiastical representations, usually Christ (IC XC) or the Virgin (MP OV) are standard for this era. Christ is generally depicted seated facing holding a book of the gospels with a hand in benediction, while the Virgin is usually *orans*. Full figures, replacing busts, are increasingly popular in both reverse and obverse types. The obverse types show the emperor, often standing in armor, and sometimes in the company of a member of the Holy Family. The legends on both sides of the coins assume the vertical form, usually split on each side of the emperor's figure with the imperial name to the left and the remainder of the titles to the right. Reverse legends are often very short and restricted to abbreviations. In some cases, the reverse types consist of representations of members of the ruling family as demonstrated by a coin of Romanus IV where the three sons of the empress, Eudocia, are standing facing. The scyphate form is believed to have originated in the reign of Isaac I of this era and persisted well into the last period of Byzantine coinage. In some reigns, both flat and scyphate coins were struck simultaneously in all metals. To all intents and purposes, mint marks and the dating of coins are no longer apparent. The "Lord Help" legend (KE ROHOEI)

REPRESENTATIVE OBVERSE LEGENDS OF THE
COMNENIAN PERIOD

Isaac I, 1057-1059
   1. ✝ICAAKIOC RACIAEV PWM
Constantine X, 1059-1067   ✝ΘKERO
   1. ✝KWN RACA O ΔOVKAC   2. HΘEIKWN
Constantine X with Eudocia   CTANTINW
Makrembolitissa   ΔECΠOTH
   1. ✝KWNTAK EVΔK AVΓO   TWΔꞰKA
   (on right) (on left)
Romanus IV, 1067-1071   ✝KC
   1. PWM   2. BOPWMA
                      NWΔECΠO
Romanus IV with Eudocia   ϹHTWΔIO
Makrembolitissa   ΓENƐI
   1. IWMAN S EVΔKAI
   2. ✝PWMAN S EVΔVKIA
Michael VII, 1071-1078   ✝K̄ER̄Θ
   1. ✝MIXAHΛ RACIΛ O Δ 2. MIXAHΛ
Michael VII with wife Maria   ΔECΠOTH
   1. ✝MIXAHΛ S MAPIA   TWΔOV
Nicephorus III, 1078-1081   KA
   1. ✝NIKH☿P' ΔEC Π
   2. ✝NIKH☿ ΔEC TW ROTANIATH
Alexius I, 1081-1118
   1.   ✝ΘKE   2. Λ   TW
       ROHΘEI   Λ Ɛ   KO
       AΛEϹIW   ϹIW   MN-I
       ΔEC'ΠOT   ΔEC   N
       TW KOM   ΠO
       NHNW   T

   3. ✝ΛΛEZIW ΔEC
   4. ✝AΛEZIW ΔECΠOT TW KOMNHNW
John II, 1118-1143   3. ĪW   ΦΛ 4. ⅃ᴎ̄
   1. ✝IW ΔECΠOTH TW ΠOPΦVPOΓNT ΔEC PO   Ǫ
   2. IW ΔECΠOT   ΠOT ΓE   Γ
                         TW NH
Manuel I, 1143-1180   Π OP   T
   1. MA   TW̄
   NꝎHΛ ΠOP
   Δ GC Φ̄V   2. MANꝎHΛ ΔECΠOT
   ΠO   POΓ
    T   MNH
       δ

REPRESENTATIVE OBVERSE LEGENDS OF THE
COMNENIAN PERIOD

Andronicus I, 1183-1185
  1. ANΔPONIKOC ΔECΠOTHC

                                  Λ
2.   AN   Є
       ΔP   Π
       I   T

Isaac II, 1185-1195
  1. ICAAKIOC ΔECΠ
Alexius III, 1195-1203
   1. AΛCȜ ΔE
   2. ΛΛCZIW KШNJA

REPRESENTATIVE REVERSE
LEGENDS

Common to all reigns
1. ✠IhS XIS REX REϚNANT Ihm
2. I̅C̅ X̅C̅ (abbreviation for Jesus Christ)
3. M̅ Θ̅ or M̅P̅ Θ̅V̅ (abbreviation for Mother of God)
Reverse legends restricted to certain reigns
 Romanus IV with Eudocia and her family
  1. ЄVΔOKI BACIΛ
  2. ✠ΘKE ROHΘЄI TW CWΔOVΛ
  3. KWN MX ANΔ (Eudocia's three sons standing)
Michael VII with wife Maria
  1. ЄN TOVTW NIKATE MIXAHΛ KAI MAPIA
Alexius I
  1. ✠ЄMMA NOVH   in field I̅C̅ X̅C̅
  2. ✠KE ROHΘЄI   around seated Christ (also used by
John II and Manuel I)
  1. C   Φ   (in cross of equal limbs)
     A Λ Δ

       A   Δ
  2. K   Φ   (cross on step)
  3. ✠KEPO ΛΛCZIW   (Christ seated)
Manuel I
     O   Nȣ   2.   O   N
  1. ЄM   HΛ (IC XC in field)   Є   ȣ   (IC XC in field)
     MA   M   H
                        M   Λ
Andronicus I   A
  1. ✠ΘKE BOHΘЄI
Isaac II   2.   3.
  1. O   X   Є   N   OЄ   Nȣ
     X   M̅I̅ (Bust of St.   M   ȣ   or   MM   HΛ
   ʼ   Ꝓ   Michael)   M   H   A
Alexius III   A   Λ   (Bust of Christ)
     O
1. ⌐Є ⌐I   2. ✠KЄRO ΛΛЄ ⟩
     Ꝓ OC

as a reverse type was introduced during this period although it attained greater popularity in the later Paleologian period.

After many centuries in jeweled court dress, the emperor again in this era begins to wear armor and shows himself in warlike attitudes. This is very characteristic of a nation which is torn with foreign aggression in which there is a great desire to stimulate the military attitude of the people. The many years of comparative internal peace of the empire were over and the Turkish invasions were in full swing. From now until the final fall of Constantinople, the predominant facet of Byzantine existence will be military and will be reflected in the coinage.

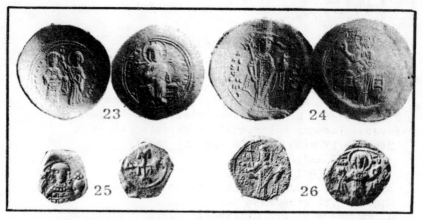

Fig. 23.   Gold Scyphate Nomisma of Constantine X. The Virgin is shown crowning the emperor on the obverse while Christ is shown seated facing on the reverse.

Fig. 24.   Gold Scyphate Nomisma of Alexius I.

Fig. 25.   Small Flat Bronze Coin of Manuel I.

Fig. 26.   Small Bronze Coin of Isaac II. The Virgin, ORANS, is the reverse type.

The standing figure of the emperor on the obverse can usually be differentiated from any saintly companions by the fact that he usually stands to the left of the field and often is crowned. The figure of a saint, Christ, or the Virgin is shown on the right and is always nimbate. Sometimes a saint may also be in armor, never the other two. In addition, if the figures are Christ or the Virgin, their monograms (IC XC, MP OV) will be shown somewhere in the field.

PART I. BYZANTIUM

HISTORICAL OUTLINE OF THE PALEOLOGIAN PERIOD

Although the coinages of neither the "Latin" empire established by the members of the Fourth Crusade nor the Greek "splinter empires" that arose in the former provinces of Byzantium are considered in this paper, some historical discussion of them is necessary to bridge the gap between the fall of Constantinople in 1204 and the re-establishment of the empire in 1261 when the troops of Michael Paleologus seized the city from the last of the futile "Latin" rulers, Baldwin II.

After the looting of Constantinople, the crusaders divided up the empire between themselves and organized feudal holdings with the theoretical capital at Constantinople. The Venetians, incidentally, seized the best parts of the empire, especially the Aegean islands as their share, carefully avoiding such untenable spoils as Asia Minor which still had to be conquered from the Greeks. The Fourth Crusade as far as the Republic of St. Mark was concerned was a huge financial success as their doge, Dandolo, had hoped when he instigated the capture of Constantinople. The first "Latin" emperor was

BALDWIN I (1204-1205 A.D.), a Flemming, and probably one of the more admirable characters of the Crusade. Baldwin was not destined to enjoy his new realm long since he was soon captured by the Bulgarians who swarmed into his land when the old empire had collapsed. When he died in captivity, his brother

HENRY (1205-1216 A.D.) succeeded to the throne and spent his reign in futile battles attempting to maintain his holdings. By the end of his reign, his kingdom was little more than the city of Constantinople. At his death,

PETER of COURTNEY (1216-1219 A.D.) became ruler, to be followed shortly by his son

ROBERT (1219-1228 A.D.). Robert, after a short unhappy rule, died and his brother

BALDWIN II (1228-1261 A.D.) became emperor of a phantom empire. He spent his long reign essentially waiting to see which of the Greek "splinter empires" would seize his capital. After the city was lost in 1261, Baldwin spent the rest of his life wandering around Europe, an empireless emperor, looking for someone to assist him to regain his throne and becoming the theme of many a mournful ballad.

THEODORE I (1204-1222 A.D.)* of the House of Lascaris was one of

---

*Formally crowned Emperor of the Romans in 1206.

the better generals at the final siege of Constantinople, keeping his troops in order until the last. He escaped from the city and fled to Nicaea where he organized the resistance to the "Latins" who attempted to invade that portion of the old empire. Theodore was not only able to hold his land against the "Latins" but also held off the Turks, who tried to take advantage of the disruption of the Greek nation. Theodore was followed by

JOHN III (1222-1254 A.D.) Ducas Vatatzes, his son-in-law who carried out his father-in-law's policies. The Empire of Nicaea, as it is now called, considered itself the legitimate successor to the old Byzantine Empire and in fact its rulers are listed chronologically by historians with the Byzantine series. Thus John III is considered as the successor in line to John II Comnenus. John tried hard to establish a solid nation and to a large degree he succeeded. He even raised chickens to help the finances of the country. On his death, his son

THEODORE II (1254-1258 A.D.) became emperor and continued his father's strong government, until his untimely death in 1258 A.D. He was succeeded by his young son

JOHN IV (1258-1259 A.D.) who was soon brought under the influence of one of his generals

MICHAEL (1260-1261 A.D.) Paleologus who had himself crowned as co-emperor and then deposed and blinded his young colleague. Michael then proceeded against the remains of the Latin power and in 1261 was able to retake Constantinople from Baldwin II. Michael then proclaimed the re-establishment of the "Roman Empire" and himself

MICHAEL VIII (1261-1282 A.D.), emperor. Although an extremely clever man, Michael was not especially strong and although he was able to hold back the various enemies of Byzantium by intrigue, he was not able to create permanent protection for his nation. He made one fatal mistake that eventually cost the empire Asia Minor when he disbanded the border guards whom he suspected (with good reason) of remaining loyal to the deposed John IV. The imperial troops were not numerous enough to guard all the passes and the Turks were able to gradually infiltrate the country. Michael's son

ANDRONICUS II (1282-1328 A.D.) was an especially inept person to attain the throne at a time when strength and intelligence were paramount for Byzantine survival. Andronicus not only was a physical coward but lacked his father's diplomatic skill. His only claim to fame was his great religious orthodoxy which did little except involve him in petty ecclesiastical squabbles. Andronicus crowned his son

MICHAEL IX (1295-1320 A.D.) co-emperor but allowed him little influence in the government which was unfortunate since Michael was made of better stuff than his father. After Michael died, his son

ANDRONICUS III (1328-1341 A.D.) rebelled against his grandfather and forced him to retire. Andronicus was not a coward and met the Turks personally on many a battlefield. However, courage was not the principal required trait in a Byzantine emperor at this late date and he was forced to see the last Asian provinces fall into their hands. The empire was on its deathbed when his son

JOHN V (1341-1391 A.D.) succeeded as emperor, he was forced to accept a position as vassal to the Turkish sultan. The fact that the sultan did not seize Constantinople several times during the next years was not because he was unable to do so, so divided and weak were the Greeks. John was troubled, even at this late date, with an usurper

JOHN VI (1341-1354 A.D.) Cantacuzenus, one of his advisers who attempted to seize the throne. John was able to hold his own in a series of storybook escapades and finally deposed his unwanted colleague. Then one of John V's sons

ANDRONICUS IV (1376-1379 A.D.) usurped his father's place when John was absent from Constantinople and maintained himself for a while in the capital. Finally, John regained his place and designated his younger son

MANUEL II (1391-1423 A.D.) as his successor. In happier times, Manuel would have probably attained fame as a great ruler. Under the circumstances, he was relegated to the task of keeping a corpse warm. Manuel is supposed to have once said that the size of the Byzantine empire no longer indicated a need for an emperor to administer the government but better a municipal magistrate. Manuel, however, during a series of civil wars between the Turks, was actually able to obtain several strips of territory as payment for his support. By always being able to sense which side was winning, he was allowed to retain his gains for some years until the grateful sultan whom he had assisted died. Manuel tried hard to obtain aid from the west and even visited France

Fig. 27.   Gold Scyphate Nomisma of Michael VIII. The reverse type is that of the Virgin praying amid the walls of Constantinople. (A.N.S. Collection).

Fig. 28.   Gold Scyphate Nomisma of Andronicus II and Michael IX. The emperors are depicted standing on either side of Christ, Andronicus, the senior ruler, to Christ's right (the left side of the obverse) while Michael is to the right of the obverse side (A.N.S.).

Fig. 29.   Flat silver coin of John VIII. Christ is shown on the reverse face. (A.N.S. Collection).

Michael VIII, 1261-1282

	X	M			X̄		3. MIXAHΛ ΔЄϹП ΔΗΜ
1.	M	I̅C̅	X̅C̅	2.	M		
	ΛC	OΠ			Δes		
	ΠC	N			Π	4. MXˣΠA	
					O		
					T		
					C		

Andronicus II, 1282-1328

1. ANΔPONIKOC

2. ANΔPONIK AVTOKPAT

Andronicus with his son
 Michael IX, 1295-1320

1. ANΔPONIVKOC MIXAHΛΔΕϹ Π

2.

	A	M
	N	I
	Δ	X
	P	A
	H Λ	

3.

A	O
N Δ	Π
PON	A
IKS	Λ
ΔЄϹ	Є
ΠOT	OΛ

Andronicus with grandson Andronicus III
1. AVTOKPATOPЄS PΩMAIWN
2. ANΔPINIKO ΔЄϹПOΤΗC
3. ANΔPONIK Λ/ΔPONII
Andronicus III, 1338-1341
1. ANΔPONIKOC ΔЄϹПOΤΗC   2. ANΔOV
John V, 1341-1391
1. IWANHC ΔЄϹПOΤΗC   2. IΘN   3.

IW
CN
XW
TW

Andronicus IV, 1376-1379
(usurper in reign of John V)
1. ANΔN   2. ANΔ
Manuel II, 1391-1423
1. ⴕ O MANOVHA OΠAΛЄOΛOΓC ΔЄϹПOT   2.

MA	ΠA
N ♂	ΛIO
HΛ	ΛO
ΔЄϹ	ΓO
ΠOT	C

John VII, 1399-1402
1. ⴕIW ΔЄϹПO OΛOΓOCN
John VIII, 1423-1448
1.   The following inscription arranged in two lines
around bust of John :
     ⴕ IW ΔЄϹПOTIC O ΠAΛЄOOΓOC
   ΘV XAPIT BACIΛЄC TWN PΩMAI

REPRESENTATIVE REVERSE LEGENDS OF THE PALEOLOGIAN PERIOD

Common to all reigns

1. $\overline{\text{IC}}$ $\overline{\text{XC}}$ (always with figure of Christ)
2. $\overline{\text{M}}$ $\overline{\Theta}$ or $\overline{\text{MP}}$ $\overline{\Theta V}$ (always with figure of Virgin)
3. Variations of the "Lord Help" legend:

ǂθKЄ ROHΘC

4. ⊢⊣

5. **ƌƁ**

Reverse legends restricted to certain reigns

Michael VIII

1.
   O   NI   (St. Nicholas)
   AΓI   KO
   OS   ΛΑ
   X

2.
   O   Θ
   A   ЄO
   ΓI   △
   (St. Theodore)

Andronicus II

1.
   △
   MI   (St. Demetrius)

3. ǂBOΘΘЄI (around a cross)

2. Ụ AΓIOCΓЄOPΓ(St. George)

Andronicus II with Michael IX

1.
   Ⓐ
   NI   A̲C̲   (St. Nicholas)
   K

2.
   Γ   NI
   Ⓐ   KO
   Ɨ Γ   ΛΑ
   O
   (St. Nicholas)

3. BO HΘCI KVPIЄ (Christ)

Andronicus II and Andronicus III

1. ǂKVPIЄ CWC ON TW C BACIΛЄIC
2. ǂAVTOKPAT Ɛ̲ PWMAIWN (with cross pattee)
3.
   AVTO
   KPATOP
   ЄCPWM
   AIWN

4.
   O   Λ
   Λ Γ   PO
   HOC   ИI
   ΛN   KO
   (St. Andronicus)

5. OΛ ΘЄOΔWPOC (St. Theodore)

6. NIΩ

John V

1.
   A   ΓI   (St. George)
   ΓI   S
   OS

2. O AΓHOC ΔMHTPIOC (St. Demetrius)

Andronicus IV

1.
   IC   XC   (arranged in the angles
   NI   AK   of cross)

and Italy. During his absence, he placed his cousin

JOHN VII (1399-1402 A.D.) on the throne as regent. When Manuel returned, John resumed his private station. Manuel was succeeded by his son

JOHN VIII (1423-1448 A.D.) who was able to do little against the Turkish encroachments. At the death of John, the succession went to his younger brother, Constantine, who had been the Despot of the Morea, the only major piece of territory still in Byzantine hands.

CONSTANTINE XI (1448-1453 A.D.) was probably the finest of the Paleologi, courageous, intelligent, and forgiving. It was unfortunate that he had to come to power when there was little left to do but die in a befitting manner. The Turkish sultan, Mohammed II, at that time finally decided to take Constantinople for his capital and there was little Constantine XI could do to prevent him. Although he asked western aid, he received little from Italy although both Venice or Genoa could probably have saved the city which by this time it was to their benefit to do. The Byzantine commercial power had been destroyed in 1204 and now the city was merely an excellent way station for the Italians. Most historians feel that they did not realize the seriousness of the situation and hence failed to act. Mohammed picked a quarrel with Constantine over a trifle and in 1452 began preparations for the siege. In spite of hard fighting by the emperor and his few assistants (the bulk of the populace stayed aloof because the Paleologi had accepted Catholicism in an effort to win western aid), the Turks were able to breach the walls on the 29th of May, 1453, and enter the city. The last emperor died in the breach in a manner fitting the spiritual successor of Trajan and Basil II. Thus, five hundred years ago this year (1953), the Turks entered Constantinople and ended one of the longest tales of empire known to the Christian world.

SUMMARY OF COINAGE IN THE PALEOLOGIAN PERIOD

Ecclesiastical representations replace all others in this dying period of the Byzantine empire. Christ and the Virgin are found on the coins of all reigns and many saints are introduced as standard reverse types and are commonly found as obverse types in company with the emperor. St. Michael appears in the reign of Michael VIII, St. George in the reign of Andronicus II, St. Demetrius in the reign of Andronicus III. A very popular obverse type is one of these Saints, or even the Virgin or Christ, crowning the emperor. A favorite reverse type used by Andronicus and his succssors is the Virgin standing in the confines of the walls of Constantinople. The coinage is cruder than in the previous reigns and, as noted previously, gold is scarce. The types and inscriptions are all Greek in character and the divided vertical style of the last period is commonly used although a few circular inscriptions may still be found. The scyphate form is used commonly until the reign of Manuel II when a flat coinage was introduced. The workmanship is generally poorer than that of the Comnenian period. Gold is very scarce except in the very early reigns of the period.

APPENDIX I. EAST ROMAN MINT MARKS

ALEXANDRIA-	ALE, AΛΕΞ	MILAN -	MD
ANTIOCH	- ANT, ANTIX, THEUP'	NICOMEDIA -	NIKO
CARTHAGE	- CAR, KARV, KRTS	RAVENNA -	RAVENNA, RAV
CATINA	- CAT	ROME -	R, ROM, RM
CHERSON	- XЄPCWNOC	SICILY -	SCLS, SCL
CONSTANTINOPLE	- CON, CONOB	SIRMIUM -	SIRM
CYPRUS	- KVΠP	SYRACUSE -	CVRAKOVCI
CYZICUS	- KYZ	THESSALONICA -	TES, ΘЄC
ISAURIA	- ISAR	TREVES -	TR

Rome, Con stantinople, and Carthage all us ed the mint mark "CONOB" on gold coin s, especially solidi.
Carthage mint also us ed the mark "CONOS" on silver coins.

APPENDIX II. UNUSUAL BYZANTINE COIN TYPES

I. The early Isaurian emperors issued a series of bronze coins bearing identical legends but with variations in type. Attribution can be made only by noting the presence of beards on the emperors figures accompanying the legends. The common obverse and reverse legends a re:

1. Leo III with son Constantine: Obverse, a bearded bust of Leo with legend I; Reverse, beardless bust with legend II.
2. Constantine V with Leo III (deceased): Obverse, bearded bust with legend II; Revers e, bearded bust with legend I.
3. Constantine V with son Leo IV: Obverse, bearded bus t with legend II; Reverse, beardless bust with legend I.

II. Se e notes on Common Byzantine Bronze Coins for information on the "anonymous series".

APPENDIX III. BYZANTINE LETTER FORMS USED IN LEGENDS

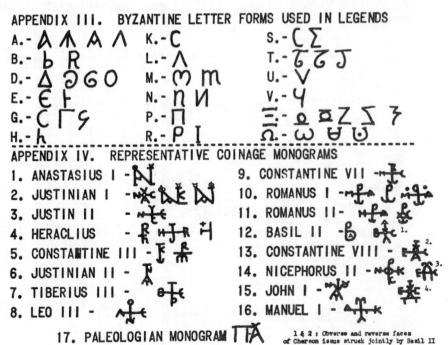

APPENDIX IV. REPRESENTATIVE COINAGE MONOGRAMS

1. ANASTASIUS I
2. JUSTINIAN I
3. JUSTIN II
4. HERACLIUS
5. CONSTANTINE III
6. JUSTINIAN II
7. TIBERIUS III
8. LEO III

9. CONSTANTINE VII
10. ROMANUS I
11. ROMANUS II
12. BASIL II
13. CONSTANTINE VIII
14. NICEPHORUS II
15. JOHN I
16. MANUEL I

17. PALEOLOGIAN MONOGRAM

1 & 2 : Obverse and reverse faces of Cherson issue struck jointly by Basil II and Constantine VIII.
3 & 4 : Reverse types of Cherson mint.

APPENDIX V.-A THEODOSIAN PERIOD DENOMINATION, RULER, MINT, AND INSCRIPTION ORIENTATION TABLES

Legends and inscriptions, Types

Legends and inscriptions, Types	ARCADIUS Solidus	Semissis	Tremissis	Siliqua	Half Siliqua	AE 1	AE 2	AE 3	AE 4	EUDOXIA Solidus	Semissis	Tremissis	Siliqua	AE 3	THEODOSIUS II Solidus	Semissis	Tremissis	AE 3	AE 4	EUDOCIA Solidus	Semissis	Tremissis	Siliqua	MARCIAN Solidus	Semissis	Tremissis	AR Coinage	AE 4
CONCORDIA AVGG (G)																												
Rome seated	X							X							X		X											
Rome seated holding shield	X																											
Rome seated inscribing shield	X																											
Cross																												
CONCORDIA MILITVM (3 soldiers)								X									X											
FELICITER NVBTIIS (3 standing figures)							X								X									X				
GLOR ORVIS TERRAR (TERRAE)																												
Emperor standing facing																												
GLORIA ROMANORVM																												
Emperor standing						X																						
3 emperors standing facing							X																					
Emperor on horseback							X																					
Emperor with captive						X	X																					
Victory walking to right																												
GLORIA REIPVBLICAE																												
Constantinople and Rome seated													X															
Empress seated																												
Camp gate								X																				
INVICTA ROMA (Walking Victory)																												
IMP XXXXII COS XVII P P (Rome seated)													X							X								
IMP XXXII COS VII P P (Rome seated)																												
SALVS AVGG (Emperor on ship with 2 captives)						X																						
SALVS REIPVBLICAE																												
Rome and Constantinople seated																												
Seated Victory																												
Seated Victory inscribing shield										X	X	X	X															
Emperor standing facing																												
Emperor with captive								X																				
2 seated facing emperors											X																	
Christogram in wreath																												
SAL REI PVI (in wreath)																												X
SALVS R PVBLICA (Emperor standing)																												
SALVS ORIENTIS FELICITAS OCCIDENTIS (Christogram)										X																		
TOV VIMV MTI (in wreath)																												
VICTORIA AVGG (G)																												
Emperor standing facing																											X	
Emperor seated facing																												
Emperor with captive	X											X																
2 emperors seated facing	X																											
VICTORIA AVGG (G)																												
Victory standing																			X									
Victory seated																										X		
Victory walking			X	X			X												X				X					
Victory standing holding long cross							X												X			X						
Seated Victory inscribing shield												X					X											
Christogram in wreath																												
VICTORIA AVGVSTORVM																												
Victory standing																												
Victory walking		X																										
Victory holding shield		X											X											X				
VIRT EXERC ROM (Emperor with captive)																												
VIRTVS AVGG (Emperor on ship with captives)					X							X																
VIRTVS AGVSTI (Emperor standing)																												
VIRTVS EXERCITI (EXERIT)																												
Emperor crowned by Victory					X																							
Emperor with captive																												
VIRTVS ROMANORVM (Rome seated)		X																										
VOT V (in wreath)								X																				
VOT V MVLT X (in wreath)			X																									
VOT X MVLT XV (in wreath)			X																									
VOT V MVLT XX (in wreath)			X																									
VOT XX MVLT XXX (in wreath)			X																									
Victory holding a long cross													X						X									
VOT XXX MVLT XXXX (in wreath)													X					X										
Rome Seated												X					X											
2 emperors seated facing												X					X											
VOT MVLT XXXX (in wreath)																X												X
VRBS ROMA (FELIX) (Rome seated)		X		X																								
Cross in wreath (no legend)							X											X		X	X	X					X	
Christogram in wreath (no legend)								X	X								X		X	X	X						X X
Monogram of ruler (no legend)																	X											X X
Trophy of arms (no legend)													X															
Emperor standing or soldier standing (no legend)																												
Emperor with captive (no legend)																												
Lion (no legend)																												
Eagle (no legend)																												
Victory walking (no legend)																												
Soldier on prow of vessel (no legend)																												
NOVA SPES REIPVBLICAE (Seated Victory)	X																											
VT XXX V (in wreath)																	X					X						

Legends and inscriptions, Types — coinage matrix by ruler and denomination.

The columns across the top, left to right, are grouped by ruler with denomination sub-columns:

PULCHERIA: Solidus, Semissis, Tremissis, AR Coinage, AE 3 — **LEO 1**: Solidus, Semissis, Tremissis, AR Coinage, AE 4, AE 2 — **VERINA**: Solidus, Tremissis, AE 2 — **LEO II & ZENO** — **ZENO**: Solidus, Semissis, Tremissis — **ZENO (alone)**: Solidus, Semissis, Tremissis, AR Coinage, AE 1, AE 3, AE 4 — **ARIADNE**: Solidus, Tremissis — **BASILISCUS**: Solidus, Semissis, Tremissis, AR Coinage, AE 4

Legends and inscriptions, Types	PULCHERIA Sol	Sem	Trem	AR	AE3	LEO 1 Sol	Sem	Trem	AR	AE4	AE2	VERINA Sol	Trem	AE2	LEO II & ZENO	ZENO Sol	Sem	Trem	ZENO(alone) Sol	Sem	Trem	AR	AE1	AE3	AE4	ARIADNE Sol	Trem	BASILISCUS Sol	Sem	Trem	AR	AE4
CONCORDIA AVGG (G)					X						X			X	X				X			X			X			X				X
Rome seated					X						X			X	X				X			X			X			X				X
Rome seated holding shield					X						X			X	X				X			X			X			X				X
Rome seated inscribing shield					X						X			X	X				X			X			X			X				X
Cross											X				X				X			X			X			X				X
CONCORDIA MILITVM (3 soldiers)					X						X			X	X				X			X			X			X				X
FELICITER NVBTIIS (3 standing figures)					X	X					X			X	X				X			X			X			X				X
GLOR ORVIS TERRAR (TERRARL)					X	X					X			X	X				X			X			X			X				X
Emperor standing facing					X						X			X	X				X			X			X			X				X
GLORIA ROMANORVM					X						X			X	X				X			X			X	X		X				X
Emperor standing					X						X			X	X				X			X			X	X		X				X
3 emperors standing facing					X						X			X	X				X			X			X			X				X
Emperor on horseback					X						X			X	X				X			X			X			X				X
Emperor with captive					X						X			X	X				X			X			X			X				X
Victory walking to right					X						X			X	X				X			X	X		X			X				X
GLORIA REIPVBLICAE					X						X			X	X				X			X			X			X				X
Constantinople and Rome seated					X						X			X	X				X			X			X			X				X
Regress seated					X						X			X	X				X			X			X			X				X
Camp gate					X						X			X	X				X			X			X			X				X
INVICTA ROMA (Walking Victory)	X				X						X			X	X				X			X			X			X				X
IMP XXXXII COS XVII P P (Rome seated)	X				X						X			X	X				X			X			X			X				X
IMP XXXII COS VII P P (Rome seated)				X	X						X			X	X				X			X			X			X				X
SALVS AVGGG (Emperor on ship with 2 captives)					X						X			X	X				X			X			X			X				X
SALVS REIPVBLICAE					X						X			X	X				X			X			X			X				X
Rome and Constantinople seated				X	X						X			X	X				X			X			X			X				X
Seated Victory				X	X						X			X	X				X			X			X			X				X
Seated Victory inscribing shield	X			X	X						X			X	X				X			X			X	X		X				X
Emperor standing facing				X	X						X			X	X				X			X			X			X				X
Emperor with captive				X	X						X			X	X				X			X			X			X				X
2 seated facing emperors				X	X						X			X	X				X			X			X			X				X
Christogram in wreath				X	X						X			X	X				X			X			X			X				X
SAL REI PVI (in wreath)					X	X					X			X	X				X			X			X			X				X
SALVS R PVBLICA (Emperor standing)					X	X					X			X	X				X			X			X			X				X
SALVS ORIENTIS FELICITAS OCCIDENTIS (Christogram)					X						X			X	X				X			X	X		X			X				X
TOV VINV NTI (in wreath)					X						X			X	X				X			X			X			X				X
VICTORIA AVGG (G)				X	X						X			X	X				X			X			X			X				X
Emperor standing facing				X	X						X			X	X				X			X			X			X				X
Emperor seated facing				X	X						X			X	X				X			X			X			X				X
Emperor with captive				X	X						X			X	X				X			X			X			X				X
2 emperors seated facing				X	X						X			X	X				X			X			X			X				X
VICTORIA AVGG (G)				X										X					X			X				X		X				
Victory standing				X										X					X			X				X		X				
Victory seated				X		X								X					X			X				X		X				
Victory walking				X										X					X			X				X		X				
Victory standing holding long cross	X			X		X						X		X		X			X			X		X	X	X		X				X
Seated Victory inscribing shield				X										X					X			X				X		X				
Christogram in wreath				X										X					X			X				X		X				
VICTORIA AVGVSTORVM				X										X					X			X				X		X				
Victory standing				X		X								X					X			X				X		X			X		
Victory walking				X										X					X	X		X		X		X		X				
Victory holding shield				X										X					X			X				X		X				
VIRT RESC ROM (Emperor with captive)				X										X					X			X				X		X				
VIRTVS AVGGG (Emperor on ship with captives2)				X										X					X			X				X		X				
VIRTVS AGVSTI (Emperor standing)				X										X					X			X				X		X				
VIRTVS EXERCITI (EXCERIT)				X										X					X			X				X		X				
Emperor crowned by Victory				X								X		X					X			X				X		X				
Emperor with captive				X										X					X			X				X		X				
VIRTVS ROMANORVM (Rome seated)				X										X					X			X				X		X				
VOT V (in wreath)				X										X					X			X				X		X				
VOT V NVLT X (in wreath)				X										X					X			X				X		X				
VOT X NVLT XV (in wreath)				X										X					X			X				X		X				
VOT V NVLT XX (in wreath)				X										X					X			X				X		X				
VOT XX NVLT XXX (in wreath)				X										X					X			X				X		X				
Victory holding a long cross	X			X										X					X			X				X		X				
VOT XXX NVLT XXXX (in wreath)				X										X					X			X				X		X				
Rome seated				X										X					X			X				X		X				
2 emperors seated facing				X										X					X			X				X		X				
VOT NVLS XXXX (in wreath)				X										X					X			X				X		X				
VRBS ROMA (FELIX) (Rome seated)			X X				X				X			X					X	X		X				X		X			X	
Cross in wreath (no legend)		X												X					X			X				X		X				X
Christogram in wreath (no legend)										X				X					X			X				X		X				
Monogram of ruler (no legend)						X								X					X			X		X		X		X				
trophy of arms (no legend)														X					X			X				X		X				
Emperor standing or soldier standing (no legend)						X								X					X			X		X		X		X				
Emperor with captive (no legend)						X								X					X			X				X		X				
Lion (no legend)						X								X					X			X			X	X		X				
Eagle (no legend)														X					X			X				X		X				
Victory walking (no legend)														X					X			X		X		X		X				
Soldier on prow of vessel (no legend)														X					X			X				X		X				X
NOVA SPES REIPVBLICAE (Seated Victory)														X					X			X				X		X				
VX XXX V (in wreath)														X					X			X				X		X				

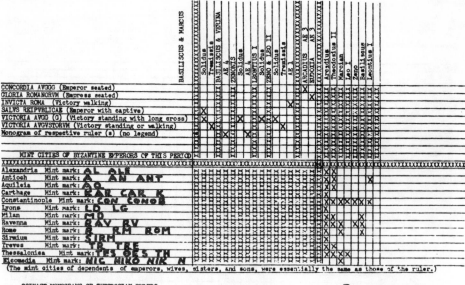

	BASILISCUS & MARCUS	Solidus	Tremissis	BASILISCUS & VERINA	AE 4	ZENONIS	Solidus	AE 4	LEONTIVS I	Solidus	ZENO & LEO II	Solidus	Tremissis	AE 1	ARCADIVS AE 3	EVDOXIA	Arcadius AE 3	Theodosius II	Marcian	Leo I	Zeno	Basiliscus	Leontius I
CONCORDIA AVGGG (Emperor seated)																							
GLORIA ROMANORVM (Empress seated)																							
INVICTA ROMA (Victory walking)																							
SALVS REIPVBLICAE (Emperor with captive)																							
VICTORIA AVGG (G) (Victory standing with long cross)																							
VICTORIA AVGVSTORVM (Victory standing or walking)																							
Monogram of respective ruler(s) (no legend)																							

MINT CITIES OF BYZANTINE EMPERORS OF THIS PERIOD

Mint	Mint mark		
Alexandria	AL	ALE	
Antioch	AN	ANT	
Aquileia	AQ		
Carthage	KAR	CAR	K
Constantinople	CON	CONOB	
Lyons	LD	LG	
Milan	MD		
Ravenna	RAV	RV	
Rome	R	RM	ROM
Sirmium	SIRM		
Treves	TR	TRE	
Thessalonica	TES	GES	TH
Nicomedia	NIC	NIKO	NIK	N

(The mint cities of dependents of emperors, wives, sisters, and sons, were essentially the same as those of the ruler.)

COINAGE MONOGRAMS OF THEODOSIAN RULERS

ARCADIUS: none listed
EUDOXIA: none listed

THEODOSIUS II:

F'DOCIA : none listed

MARCIAN:

PULCHERIA: none listed

LEO I:

VERINA : none listed
LEO II : none listed

ZENO:

ARIADNE : none listed

BASILISCUS :

BASILISCUS & VERINA :

ZENONIS :

APPENDIX V-B   FIVE NUMMIA DENOMINATION REVERSES, "E" TYPES

JUSTINIAN I
Obverse: Diademed bust facing right for 1,2,3,4
Constantinople   Cyzicus   Carthage

Obv: Monogram for 5,6
Non Imperial types

ANASTASIUS I
Obv: Diademed bust facing right.
Constantinople (7) Antioch (8,9)

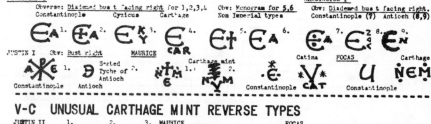

JUSTIN I   Obv: Bust right   MAURICE

Constantinople   Antioch

Catina   FOCAS   Carthage

Constantinople   Constantinople

V-C   UNUSUAL CARTHAGE MINT REVERSE TYPES

JUSTIN II   1.   2.   3.   MAURICE   FOCAS

10 NUMMIA   10 NUMMIA   10 NUMMIA   20 NUMMIA   10 NUMMIA   10 NUMMIA   20 NUMMIA

HERACLIUS   CONSTANTINE III

1.   2.   1.   2.   3.   4.

20 NUMMIA   10 NUMMIA   20 NUMMIA   40 NUMMIA   20 NUMMIA   10 NUMMIA

Obverses are all facing bust types except t some issues of Justin.

V-D   COMNENIAN COMMON BRONZE COINS

ALEXIUS I   1.   2.

Reverse types
Obv: Facing bust of Alexius

Alexius, John II, and Manuel I all struck small bronze coins with facing busts of Christ and the Virgin. Alexius' types utilizing the Virgin usually had a medallion of Christ present. John used standing figures more often than his father. The key to these coins is usually in the obverse legend (the first few letters):

Alexius: +ΑΛΕΞΙω ΔΕCΠΟΤ   John: +IW ΔΕCΠΟΤΗ   Manuel: ΜΑΝΥΗΛ ΔΕCΠ

APPENDIX VI. Chronological List of Byzantine Rulers by Dynasties

THEODOSIAN DYNASTY
Arcadius, 395-408
Theodosius II, 408-450
Marcian, 450-457
   LEONINE DYNASTY
Leo I, 457-474
Leo II, 474
Zeno, 474-491
Basiliscus (u), 476-477
Leontius (u), 484-488
Anastasius I, 491-518
   JUSTINIANEAN DYNASTY
Justin I, 518-527
Justinian I, 527-565
Justin II, 565-578
Tiberius II, 578-582
Maurice Tiberius, 582-602
Phocas (u), 602-610
   HERACLIAN DYNASTY
Heraclius, 610-641
Heraclius Constantine, 641
Heracleonas, 641
Constantine III, 641-668
Constantine IV, 668-685
Justinian II, 685-695
Leontius (u), 695-698
Tiberius III, 698-705
Justinian II, 705-711
   Non-Dynastic
Filepicus Bardanes, 711-713
Anastasius II, 713-716
Theodosius III, 716-717
   ISAURIAN DYNASTY
Leo III, 717-741
Constantine V, 741-775
Artavasdus (u), 742-744
Leo IV, 775-780
Constantine VI, 780-797
Irene, 797-802
   ARABIAN DYNASTY
Nicephorus I, 802-811
Stauracius, 811
Michael I, 811-813
Leo V (u), 813-820
   AMORIAN DYNASTY
Michael II, 820-829
Theophilus, 829-842
Michael III, 842-867
   MACEDONIAN DYNASTY
Basil I, 867-886
Leo VI, 886-912
Alexander, 886-913
Constantine VII, 913-959
Romanus I, 919-944

Romanus II, 959-963
Basil II, 963-1025
Constantine VIII, 963-1028
Nicephorus II, 963-969
John I, 969-976
Romanus III, 1028-1034
Michael IV, 1034-1041
Michael V, 1041-1042
Zoe and Theodora, 1042
Constantine IX, 1042-1055
Theodora, 1055-1056
Michael VI, 1056-1057
   Non-Dynastic
Isaac I, 1057-1059
   DUCAS DYNASTY
Constantine X, 1059-1067
Romanus IV, 1067-1071
Michael VII, 1071-1078
   Non-Dynastic
Nicephorus III, 1078-1081
   COMNENIAN DYNASTY
Alexius I, 1081-1118
John I, 1118-1143
Manuel I, 1143-1180
Alexius II, 1180-1183
Andronicus I, 1183-1185
   ANGELIAN DYNASTY
Isaac II, 1185-1195
Alexius III, 1195-1203
Isaac II and Alexius IV, 1203-1204
Alexius V (u), 1204
   LASCARIS-DUCAS DYNASTY
   (at Nicaea)
Theodore I, 1204-1222
John III, 1222-1254
Theodore II, 1254-1258
John IV, 1258-1259
   PALEOLOGIAN DYNASTY
Michael VIII, 1260-1261 (at Nicaea);
   1261-1282 (at Constantinople)
Andronicus II, 1282-1328
Michael IX, 1295-1320
Andronicus III, 1328-1341
John V, 1341-1391
John VI (u), 1341-1354
Andronicus IV (u), 1376-1379
Manuel II, 1391-1423
John VII, 1399-1402
John VIII, 1423-1448
Constantine XI, 1448-1453

Compilation based on Goodacre, Baynes
and Wroth.
("u" — usurper)

APPENDIX VII. Family and Familiar Names of Byzantine Emperors

The East Romans were extremely fond of giving their rulers nicknames based on the place of birth, their personal appearance, or on deeds they performed during their reign. This method of designating emperors is often somewhat confusing to the beginning collector who has only a slight knowledge of Byzantine history. The following tables are included in the hope that they will be of aid in identifying emperors so listed.

I. FAMILY NAMES of Byzantine Emperors

ANGELUS
   Isaac II
   Alexius III
   Alexius IV
APSIMARUS
   Tiberius III
ARGYRUS
   Romanus III
ARTEMIUS
   Anastasius II
BARDANES
   Filepicus
BOTANIATES
   Nicephorus III
CANTACUZENUS
   John VI
COMNENUS
   Isaac I
   Alexius I
   John II

   Manuel I
   Alexius II
   Andronicus I
DIOGENES
   Romanus IV
DUCAS
   Constantine X
   Michael VII
   Alexius V
DUCAS LASCARIS
   Theodore II
DUCAS VATATZES
   John III
KALAPHATES
   Michael V
LASCARIS
   Theodore I
   John IV
LECAPENUS
   Romanus I

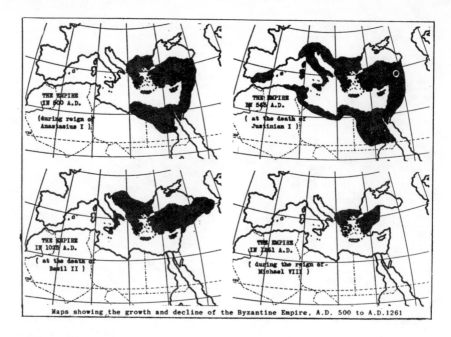

Maps showing the growth and decline of the Byzantine Empire, A.D. 500 to A.D.1261

MAKREMBOLITISSA
  Eudocia (wife of
    Constantine X)
MONOMACHUS
  Constantine IX
PALEOLOGUS
  Michael VIII
  Andronicus II
  Michael IX
  Andronicus III
  John V
  Andronicus IV

  Manuel II
  John VII
  John VIII
  Constantine XI
PHOCAS (FOCAS)
  Nicephorus II
RHANGABE
  Michael I
STRATIOTICUS
  Michael VI
ZIMISCES
  John I

II. Rulers referred to by the place of origin

ADRAMYTIUS (City in Asia Minor)
  Theodosius III
AMORIAN (Amorion, city in Asia Minor)
  Michael II
ARMENIAN
  Leo V
ATHENIAN
  Irene
ARAB (His family was believed to be of
  Arab stock)

  Nicephorus I
ISAURIAN (region in Asia Minor)
  Leo III
MACEDONIAN
  Basil I
PAPHLOGONIAN (region in Asia Minor)
  Michael IV

III. Rulers' names based on appearance or deeds

BULGAROKTONOS (Slayer of Bulgar-
  ians)
  Basil II — so named because of his
bloody victories over this nation.
COPRONYMUS
  Constantine V — so named because he
fouled the baptismal font as an infant.
DRUNKARD
  Michael III — so named because of his
fondness for loose living.
KHAZAR
  Leo IV — so named because he resem-
bled members of this tribe in appearance.
MOURTZOUPHOLOS
  Alexius V — so named because of his
bushy eyebrows.
PARAPINAKES (peck-filcher)
  Michael VII — so named because in a
famine period he reduced the measure of
grain to be purchased for one nomisma.
POGONATES (The Bearded)

  Constantine IV — so named because
when he returned to Constantinople after
succeeding to the throne he had a heavy
beard in contrast to his youthful clean
shaven appearance when he had left
the city.
PORPHYROGENITUS (Born in the Purple)
  Constantine VII — so named because of
his birth in the royal chambers of the
empress.
RHINOMETUS (Slit-nose)
  Justinian II — so named because of his
appearance on his return from exile
where his nose had been slit by order
of Tiberius III.
STAMMERER
  Michael II — so named because he possessed a marked lisp.
WISE
  Leo VI — so named because of his
scholarly achievements.

THE BYZANTINE EMPIRE A.D. 500-A.D. 1261
PRINCIPAL REFERENCES

ACKERMAN, J. 1834 *A Descriptive Catalogue of Rare and Unedited Roman Coins.* 2 volumes. Wilson, London.

BAYNES, N. 1943 *The Byzantine Empire* (in Home University Library.) Oxford University Press, London.

FINLAY, G. 1877 *A History of Greece.* 7 volumes. Clarendon Press, Oxford.

GIBBON, E. 1946 *The Decline and Fall of the Roman Empire,* ed. by J. B. Bury. 3 volumes. Heritage Press, New York.

GOODACRE, H. 1928 *Handbook to Coinage of the Byzantine Empire.* Part I. Arcadius to Leontius. Spink and Son, London.

GOODACRE, H. 1931 *Handbook to Coinage of the Byzantine Empire.* Part II Anastasius to Michael VI. Spink and Son, London.

GOODACRE, H. 1933 *Handbook to Coinage of the Byzantine Empire.* Part III. Isaac I to Constantine XI. Spink and Son, London.

HILL, G. 1899 *Handbook of Greek and Roman Coins.* MacMillan, New York.

MATTINGLY, H. 1927 *A Guide to the Exhibition of Roman Coins in the British Museum.* Oxford University Press, London.

OMAN, C. 1898 *The Byzantine Empire.* G. P. Putnam, London.

RUNCIMAN, S. 1933 *Byzantine Civilization.* Arnold Press, London.

SABATIER, J. 1862 *Description General des Monnaies Byzantines.* 2 volumes. Paris.

VASILIEV, A. A. 1952 *History of the Byzantine Empire.* University of Wisconsin Press, Madison.

WROTH, W. 1908 *Catalogue of the Imperial Byzantine Coins in the British Museum.* 2 volumes. London.

PART II. NICAEA-TREBIZOND

During the 57 years that followed their seizure of Constantinople in 1204, the "Latins" (as the western invaders were called by the Greeks) were faced with constantly increasing pressure from various Greek splinter empires which had been created in the Byzantine provinces by loyal generals who had as their principal aim the destruction of the feudal kingdoms of the Crusaders and the reestablishment of the old Byzantine Empire. Four principal empires thus created were the Despotate of Epirus, and the Empires of Thessalonica, Nicaea, and Trebizond. Each considered itself the true successor to the imperial title. Of these, the latter two were of real importance. The Nicaean Empire, although it lasted only a little over fifty years, absorbed both the Epirote Despotate and the Empire of Thessalonica. Finally in 1261, it was Nicaean troops which captured Constantinople and re-established the Byzantine nation. The Empire of Trebizond achieved its importance by virtue of the fact that it managed to exist for over two hundred and fifty years, becoming a great commercial center before falling to the Turks and outliving parent Byzantium by about eight years.

Except for a few scholarly works, the coinages of both nations have been neglected and the average collector is unaware of their existence. This is unfortunate since the coins, especially those of Trebizond, are not hard to obtain and provide excellent examples of a type of medieval currency not found elsewhere. The asper of Trebizond during its existence was one of the most important mediums of exchange in the Caucasian and Black Sea areas, while the Nicaean coins provide an excellent continuation of the Byzantine series during the years of exile.

In approaching these coinages, the same procedure that was used in Part I has been followed. First the historical outline of each empire is given, then a general discussion of coin types and inscriptions followed by a listing of representative obverse and reverse legends for each ruler. Although, as in the Byzantine section, few specific distinctions are made between coins of various metals in the tables, the reader should be able to identify the commoner Nicaean and Trebizond coins as to ruler and denomination with the aid of this paper. He should also be able to distinguish them from the very similar Byzantine coins of the Comnenian and Paleologian periods.

In all, it is hoped that this paper will serve to introduce these two fascinating series to the average collector and give him a simple means of identifying these coins that has been heretofore lacking. For those interested in studying these coinages more intensively, there is no better reference than the excellent text written by Warwick Wroth in 1911 for the British Museum. In compiling this paper, his attributions in regard to strikings, rulers, and denominations were accepted as the final authority. Although other texts were consulted, in cases of doubt, his decisions were the ones used in this compilation. The coinage of Nicaea will be considered first, followed by the more lengthy Trebizond series. A few notes regarding the coinage of the two other splinter states, Epirus and Thessalonica, are included.

HISTORICAL OUTLINE OF THE NICAEAN EMPIRE

Although the historical background of the Nicaean Empire was given in the first part, a brief review of that nation's history might be of value before considering its coinage.

THEODORE I (1204-1222 A.D.) of the house of Lascaris was one of the few Greek generals who kept his head in the confusion following the collapse of the Byzantine Empire of the Angeli under the attacks of the "Latins" of the Fourth Crusade. After Constantinople fell, Theodore with the remnants of his troops withdrew to western Asia Minor and organized the defenses of those provinces against the western invaders. Placing his capital at Nicaea, Theodore successfully defended his territories against both the "Latins" and the Turkish hordes who swarmed onto the western plains of Asia Minor when it appeared the Byzantine power was broken. Theodore allowed himself to be formally crowned in 1206 as "Emperor of the Romans" and considered himself the legitimate successor to the Byzantine throne. It was in this respect that he attacked and defeated the forces of Alexius Comnenus of Trebizond whom he regarded as an imperial usurper. Theodore died after a reign of 18 years having firmly established his Nicaean Empire as a real power in Asia Minor. He was succeeded by his energetic son-in-law

JOHN I (1222-1254 A.D.) Ducas Vatatzes. John was an extremely capable ruler and continued the aggressive policies of Theodore I. By skillful military and diplomatic manipulations he was able to incorporate the neighboring Greek splinter states of Thessalonica and Epirus into his empire, leaving the "Latins" in control of little more than Constantinople, portions of Greece, and the Aegean Islands. He also forced the Turkish sultanates back and established complete authority over western Asia Minor. At one time he even besieged Constantinople but was unable to take the city and withdrew. John was followed by his son

THEODORE II (1254-1258 A.D.) Ducas Lascaris, an intelligent and capable man. Theodore was a philosopher-emperor and labored during his short reign to improve the lot of his subjects in addition to expanding and consolidating the political gains of his father. Unfortunately, he died prematurely and his young son

JOHN II (1258-1259 A.D.) became emperor. As usual during those times, a regency meant palace intrigue and soon an unscrupulous general, Michael Paleologus, was able to have himself crowned as co-ruler

MICHAEL I (1260-1261 A.D.). Needless to say, once Michael was proclaimed emperor, John was soon deposed, blinded, and imprisoned by the ambitious general. In 1261 Nicaean troops seized Constantinople and Michael moved his government back to the old Byzantine capital. The reestablishment of the "Roman Empire" was then proclaimed and the Nicaean Empire as a distinct political entity disappeared. After Constantinople was regained in 1261, Nicaean history as such ends and the events of the succeeding years of Michael's reign are considered Byzantine and are studied as part of that nation's history.

In the chronology of the Byzantine emperors, it is customary to consider the Nicaean princes as the direct line of succession to the throne and the two Johns are listed in that series as John III and IV while Michael is considered Michael VIII. Since there were no previous emperors named Theodore, their listing as I and II is unchanged.

SUMMARY OF THE COINAGE OF THE NICAEAN EMPIRE

Nicaean coins, more so than those of Trebizond, resemble those issued by the Comnenian and early Paleologian Byzantine emperors. They are commonly scyphate (cup shaped), are struck in all three coinage metals, have the strongly ecclesiastical obverse and reverse types,

Fig. 1. Scyphate gold nomisma of John Ducas Vatatzes (John III in the Byzantine Series).

Fig. 2. Scyphate gold nomisma of Theodore II Ducas Lascaris of Nicaea.

and use the typical Byzantine vertical divided legends. The emperor is always shown on the obverse usually in the company of Christ, the Virgin, or an appropriate saint (commonly the namesake of the emperor). The identification of the coins of only three of the five Nicaean emperors raises any question, since John II did not issue coins in his own name during his brief reign and there is only one coin type of Michael that can accurately be assigned to his Nicaean reign, the bulk of his coinage being classed as Byzantine since it was issued after the recapture

REPRESENTATIVE OBVERSE LEGENDS OF THE
NICAEAN EMPIRE

Theodore I   1204-1222

(1) ΘΕΟΔWPOC ΔECΠ Ⱦ ΠΦΥΡΟΓC

(2) ΘΕΟΔWPOC (on left) ; O ΘΕΟΔWPOS (on right)

John I   1222-1254

(1)	I̅W̅		(2)	I̅W̅	Ⱦ	(3)	I̅W̅	O	
	ΔΕC	Ⱦ			Π		Δ		ᏻ
	ΠΟ	Π		ΔΕC	P		Ε		
	T	P		ΠΟ	VP			C	
	H	Φ		T	O				
				H	Γ				

Theodore II   1254-1258

(1)			(2) ΘΕΟΔWPC ΔᴕΚΑC
	ΘΕ	ΠΟ	
	ΟΔW	T͞HC	
	POC	OΛ	
	ΔΕ	K	
	C	P	

Michael   1260-1261

(1)	X	OΠ
	M	ΛΛ
		ΕΟ
		ΛΟ
		Γ
		C

REPRESENTATIVE REVERSE LEGENDS OF THE
NICAEAN EMPIRE

Legends common to the reigns of Theodore I and II, John I.

(1)

    IC XC   Monogram of Christ

(2) MP ѲV   Monogram of the Virgin

Legends found only in the reign of John I.

(1)

    Ⓐ   ΡΙ   St. Demetrius standing facing
    ΔH   in military costume.
    M   Ƨ
    ·I

(2)

    Ⓐ   Ꝺ   St. George standing facing
                   in military costume

Legends common to the reigns of Theodore II and Michael

(1)   A   St. Tryphon standing facing
      TP V   Ⱦ   holding patriarchal cross
                    (Theodore II)

(2)   Γ
    Ⓐ   Φ   St. Tryphon standing facing
    TP   W   holding a short cross
      V   N   (Michael)

of Constantinople. The use of Greek letters is standard, and ligatures, monograms, and abbreviations in the various titles are routine. The rulers of Nicaea, like their Byzantine predecessors, always use the title of "despot" and Theodore I and John I place the title "porphyrogenitus" or "born in the purple" in their obverse legends, probably to strengthen their claim that they were the legitimate successors to the Byzantine throne.

Theodore II abandoned the title "porphyrogenitus" but uses his family names of Ducas and Lascaris in his legends, the latter usually being more abridged than the former. Both of his predecessors use the surname Ducas occasionally but not in combination with Lascaris. Theodore, on his gold, shows himself in the company of the Virgin on the obverse, while on his silver and bronze he is partial to the company of St. Theodore. The gold obverse types of John I are similar to those of Theodore but on his silver John prefers St. Constantine as his companion, and on some pieces has selected the Christ of Chalce to stand at his left (the right of the coin). As a rule John is alone on his bronze issues. Theodore II in his gold followed tradition but on silver uses both Christ and the Virgin as companions and in a few cases stands alone. His bronze obverses are similar to those of his silver. On the obverse of the Michael's Nicaean bronze coin, he is shown standing with the Virgin.

The Nicaean reverses resemble those of Comnenian Byzantium. The figures of Christ ($\overline{\text{IC}}$ $\overline{\text{XC}}$) and the Virgin ($\overline{\text{MP}}$ $\overline{\text{OV}}$) are common. John also used St. Demetrius, St. George, and seraphs as reverse types while his son Theodore II used St. Tryphon, the patron saint of Nicaea. Michael also used St. Tryphon on the one coin attributed to his Nicaean reign.

In general, it is difficult for the beginner to distinguish a Nicaean coin from a Byzantine issue by the reverse alone. In most cases, the key to identification is the obverse legend containing the imperial name and titles.

HISTORICAL OUTLINE OF THE EMPERORS OF TREBIZOND

In the confusion following the fall of Constantinople in 1204, Alexius Comnenus, a grandson of the old Byzantine emperor Andronicus I, managed to escape the city and make his way to the provincial capital of Trebizond. Because of his high birth, he established himself as master of the province and gathered together the local troops under his banner. Alexius then had himself crowned as "Emperor of the Romans" and announced his intention of driving the "Latins" from Constantinople and re-establishing the Byzantine empire. In fact, however, his actions had the effect of creating a new nation with himself

ALEXIUS I (1204-1222 A.D.) as the first emperor. In the beginning, Alexius did attempt to carry through his plan and sent his armies into Bythnia as a preliminary to attacking Constantinople. Unfortunately, Theodore Lascaris, the founder of the newly constituted empire of Nicaea also had the idea of being the savior of old Byzantium, and came into direct conflict with the Nicaean ruler. Theodore defeated the Trebizond armies in the initial encounters and forced them back from the Bythnian coast. Because of a sudden Turkish attack in his rear Alexius was forced to withdraw from the campaign. His forces never again attempted a reconquest of Constantinople or western Asia Minor. The wars with the Turks kept Alexius completely occupied and after a long, drawnout struggle he was forced to acknowledge himself their vassal. In spite of the turbulence of his reign, Alexius established a prosperous commercial kingdom which lasted for almost two and a half centuries. In addition to his imperial title, Alexius adopted for himself and his descendants the title of "Grand Comnenus" to distinguish his branch of the familly from that of his Byzantine ancestors. Alexius was followed by his son-in-law

ANDRONICUS I (1222-1235 A.D.). Andronicus proved to be a prudent ruler and by skilful diplomacy set aside the Turkish vassalage and established his nation as an equal to the sultanate in central Asia Minor. Their relations, however, were not always of the best and Andronicus was once forced to withstand a determined Turkish attack on his capital. The Turkish forces were severely defeated during a night attack and withdrew leaving Trebizond as an independent power. After his death in 1235, Andronicus was succeeded by his brother-in-law

JOHN I (1235-1238 A.D.) who ruled prudently for three years before being accidentally killed in a game very similar to polo called tzukanion. He was succeeded by his second son

MANUEL I (1238-1263 A.D.), called the "Great Captain." Unfortunately for Trebizond, the comparatively friendly Turkish sultan, Aladdin, who had refrained from attacking the empire since his defeat under the city's walls during the reign of Andronicus, died and the void was filled by the Mongol hordes who were then overrunning all of the near east. Although Manuel initially joined with the Turks in an effort to halt the Mongols, he was able to gain a favorable peace with them by submitting immediately after his first defeat at their hands and acknowledging himself a Mongol vassal. Little is known of the military exploits which earned him the title of "Great Captain" but considering the times and knowing that he kept his little empire intact against both Turkish and Mongol inroads, he is probably entitled to all the honors possible in this regard. In spite of the numerous invasions, Manuel's reign was prosperous and Trebizond was rapidly becoming the leading commercial center on the Black Sea. Manuel was followed as emperor by his eldest son

ANDRONICUS II (1263-1266 A.D.) who continued his father's policies with success. Andronicus died without issue after only three years and was succeeded by his brother

GEORGE (1266-1280 A.D.), the second son of Manuel I. Due to a periodic breaking up of the Turkish and Mongol empires, George was able to establish again the complete independence of Trebizond. This sudden freedom from external invasion left the country free for internal strife and George found himself fighting continually with his nobles for the actual rule of Trebizond. His end came during a campaign against the Turkomans, when he was treacherously deserted by his troops and allowed to fall into the enemy's hands. When the news of his capture reached the capital, the third son of Manuel I

JOHN II (1280-1297 A.D.) seized the throne. The empire was now completely free of foreign domination and had the new ruler been a man of ability, Trebizond might have attained real importance in the politics of Asia Minor. John, however, was a mild sovereign, and although the empire maintained an even course, no progress was made in bettering the always delicate position of the nation in regard to foreign aggression. John is best known for his marriage to the daughter of the newly constituted Byzantine emperor, Michael VIII. Michael was able to persuade John to abandon the title "Emperor of the Romans," and assume the lesser title of "Emperor of the East," leaving the old Byzantine title to Michael. John was continually bothered by civil strife and was even forced for a short period from his capital by his sister

THEODORA (1285 A.D.). Theodora was unable to hold the throne against her brother and John returned to Trebizond to complete his reign of 18 years. At his death

ALEXIUS II (1297-1330 A.D.), his eldest son, became emperor. Unlike his father, Alexius was a fairly vigorous ruler and had a successful and peaceful reign. He did have some trouble with the Genoese traders who frequented Trebizond and at one time was forced to fight an insurrection by them in his own capital, a squabble which he successfully concluded at terms most favorable for Trebizond. Alexius died after a very prosperous reign of 33 years to be succeeded by his eldest son

ANDRONICUS III (1330-1332 A.D.). As so often happens, the popular father was followed by an unpopular son. Andronicus turned out to be a tyrant whose first act was to murder two of his three younger brothers. His second brother, Basil, escaped only through a hasty departure from Trebizond at the first news of his father's death. Andronicus was succeeded after a little more than 18 months by his young son

MANUEL II (1332 A.D.) a child of only eight years. As was usual at that time, the advent of a regency was the signal for widespread intrigue within the palace. Also, after years of comparative peace the Turkomans again invaded the empire. Although the invasion was repelled, the anarchy became so alarming that Basil, the second son of Alexius II, was invited to return from Constantinople where he had taken refuge with the Byzantine emperor and assume the throne.

BASIL (1332-1340 A.D.) returned but his rule was not much improvement over that of his unfortunate nephew, and although his generals repelled the Turkoman incursions, the personal corruption of the emperor caused much resentment. Basil died in 1340 and his wife

IRENE (1340-1341 A.D.) Palaeologina, the daughter of Byzantine emperor Andronicus III, assumed the throne. Irene took after her father and apparently was a rather gay individual, though not entirely incapable. Female rule, however, especially by one who could be accused of receiving instructions from Constantinople, was not popular and Irene was soon deposed and returned home. Her successor

ANNA (1341-1342 A.D.), was the eldest daughter of Alexius II. Although Anna managed to seize the throne after Irene returned to Constantinople, she was unable to hold it and after a very short time was deposed by a palace revolution, initiated by the arrival in Trebizond of Michael Grand-Comnenus, a now elderly younger son of John II, and his 19 year old son John. Oddly enough, it was not the father but the son who was chosen for the throne and

JOHN III (1342-1344 A.D.) became emperor. His father was placed in prison as a possible source of danger to the crown and the ex-empress, as a matter of course, was immediately strangled. John was a weak ruler and after a brief reign was deposed by palace intrigue and replaced by his recently released father

MICHAEL (1344-1349 A.D.). Michael might have been a good ruler if he had succeeded to the throne years earlier, but now he was essentially a broken old man. He tried desperately to break the power of the nobles which had caused the rapid succession of rulers with its bloodshed and national instability. In this he was supported by the people of his capital but the results of his restoration of some internal tranquility were ruined by new Turkoman invasions, a plague which decimated the population. Finally an unfortunate war with the Genoese ended disastrously for Trebizond. As a result, Michael abdicated and was succeeded by

ALEXIUS III (1349-1390 A.D.) the son of Basil and Irene. Alexius was not a really strong ruler but he did control the turbulent nobility and held back the forces of his Mohammedan neighbors. He was not so successful with the Turkoman hordes and suffered several severe defeats during his long reign. All things considered, however, the reign of Alexius must be considered prosperous and his military failures of minor importance. After 41 years, the longest reign in Trebizond history, Alexius died and was succeeded by his son

MANUEL III (1390-1417 A.D.). Manuel proved to be a worthy successor to his father inheriting both his military and diplomatic talents. Shortly after his accession, Manuel had to deal with the great Tartar invasion of Asia Minor under Timor. By immediately submitting to Timor and acknowledging himself a Tartar vassal, Manuel saved his empire from devastation and simultaneously obtained a strong protector from the Turks. Manuel was not present at the great battle of Angora which temporarily destroyed the Turkish power although as a Tartar vassal he had contributed troops to the Tartar army. It might be noted that Manuel continued to miss all military engagements that were not of immediate benefit to Trebizond. He was, indeed, a true son of the house of Comnenus. At his death in 1417, his son

ALEXIUS IV (1417-1446 A.D.) became emperor. Unfortunately for Alexius, who was not a particularly strong character, the receding power of the Tartars removed the protection that Trebizond had enjoyed as a vassal state and the empire was promptly attacked by the revitalized Turkoman tribes. Alexius submitted himself as a vassal to the Black Turkomans and obtained relief from foreign attack but his family life continued to be turbulent. He was constantly threatened by palace intrigue and after one attempt on his life, his son John was actually driven from the city. In exile John instigated a civil war against his father and during a series of negotiations between Alexius and his son, the father was found stabbed to death in bed, and the late rebel

JOHN IV (1446-1458 A.D.) succeeded to the throne. Trebizond had been severely weakened by the foreign and civil wars that preceded his accession to the throne. Only a military genius could have maintained the nation's position. Although willing, John proved inept as a soldier and the steady incursions of the Turks took an increasing toll of the nation's resources. Following military failure, John turned to diplomatic means and as had happened so frequently in the past, met with some success. John visualized a Grand Alliance against the Ottoman Turks and if he had not died prematurely, he may have succeeded in forming such a union. John gathered together as allies the still independent Seljuk Turkish emirs, the Turkoman hordes that still roamed central Asia Minor, and the rugged Christian mountaineers of Caucasia. The main force of the alliance was centered in the Turkoman hordes whose light cavalry was invincible when used on the open plains. John's relations with the White Turkomans were further improved by the fact that his sister was the wife of their great khan and exercised large influence over his actions. Just as it appeared that John had actually wielded together a workable alliance that could have held the Ottomans, he died and was succeeded by his foolish and very weak brother

DAVID (1458-1461 A.D.) who had all of John's personal weakness and none of his diplomatic skill. The Grand Alliance rapidly fell apart without John's skilful hand and David was soon placed under heavy Turkish pressure. Mohammed II, the conqueror of Constantinople, decided in 1461 to add Trebizond to his dominions. When his army appeared before the city, David, in spite of a strong fortress and the immediate advent of winter which would have made a sustained siege impossible, was persuaded to surrender the city without a struggle, ending the history of Trebizond as an independent nation. It should be noted that David's cowardly conduct was of little avail since Mohammed had him murdered several years later in Constantinople on the grounds that he was conspiring with the Turkomans to re-establish his empire. The city itself was reduced to the status of a provincial Turkish town while its Christian inhabitants were mostly either enslaved or converted to the Islamic faith.

SUMMARY OF THE COINAGE OF TREBIZOND

Trebizond issued coins struck in only two metals, copper and silver, no gold coins having ever been attributed to any of its rulers. The standard unit of coinage was the silver asper, a coin first struck by John I about 1235 and at that time weighing about 44 grains and about an inch in diameter. A certain amount of depreciation took place over the years and by the end of the empire, the asper had fallen in weight to about 20 grains, although it should be noted that some experts believe that the lighter coin should be classified as a half-asper rather than an asper. Alexius II introduced a half-asper denomination which was struck simultaneously with the asper. Later, in the reign of Alexius III, even a quarter-asper was circulated. The highest weight attained by the half-asper was about 27 grains while the quarter-aspers ran about 13 grains of silver. In addition to the flat asper coinage, Manuel I struck a scyphate silver coin of 45-47 grains weight, but as it apparently was not popular with the people his successors discontinued striking the piece.

Bronze coins were struck by Manuel I, John II, Theodora, Basil, John III, Michael, Alexius III, and Manuel III. These coins were of varying size (0.6 to 1.0 inches in diameter) and, in contrast to the silver coinage, were frequently scyphate. In addition to the attributed bronze coinage, a series of anonymous bronze coins were issued in the later years of the empire, probably during the reigns of Alexius IV and his sons.

The obverse of all Trebizond coins is occupied by a crowned and elaborately robed figure of the emperor depicted standing facing until about 1297. After that date, he is shown on horseback riding to the right. An inscription containing the imperial name and the surname "Comnenus" completes the obverse. Sometimes the *manus Dei* (hand of God) is shown crowning the emperor's figure.

Although it is impossible to differentiate between the various emperors of the same name by the obverse figure alone, sometimes the way the emperor is shown depicted is typical enough to give some indication as to his identity. John I is commonly portrayed standing facing in regal robes, his right hand holding a long cross and his left a roll of parchment with one end of his long mantle falling across his left arm. Usually his full name is given in the legend, in contrast with John II whose name is generally abbreviated. The figure of Manuel I is similar to that of John I except a labarum is in his right hand. Like John I, his name is spelled out more fully than that of Manuel III, with three or more letters being given in the obverse legend. As a rule, John II holds a short shafted labarum in his right hand and in his left holds a globus crucifer in place of the parchment roll. John III, who did not issue any silver, is shown on his bronze coins standing facing, holding a triple headed scepter in his right hand and the globus in his left. The empress Theodora is the only standing figure holding the left hand across the chest. She holds the globus in her right hand.

The mounted emperors (Alexius II onward) are less distinctive than those depicted standing but some distinctions can be made by noting the type of scepter they carry. Basically, they are all seated on a horse walking to the right, their left hand on the bridle and a scepter in their right. The differentiation is made by noting the type of head on the scepter. Alexius II holds a scepter with a triple pearled head (see appendix for scepter types in detail), while his namesake Alexius III holds a three-headed, trident-like scepter. Alexius IV and Manuel III hold scepters with three bars across the top. The emperor Basil holds the triple headed variety like Alexius III, while Michael used the triple pearled type of Alexius II.

Fig. 3. Silver asper of John I of Trebizond.
Fig. 4. Silver asper of John II of Trebizond.
Fig. 5. Silver asper of Alexius II of Trebizond.

The presence of the surname Comnenus, (KOMNHNOC) usually abridged, in the obverse legend of all coins is typical of Trebizond coinage, the flatness of the coins differentiating them from the scyphate silver coinage struck by the Byzantine emperors of the same name. In the case of the bronze issues this is not so specific, but reverse types usually make differentiation fairly easy. The full surname rarely appears in the obverse legend and in many cases one or two letters are all that are present. KMN is a common abbreviation. The rulers of Trebizond did not use the title "Despot" in their obverse legends giving us another means of differentiating them from the Byzantine and Nicaean series.

The reverse, with a very few exceptions, is always that of St. Eugenius, the patron saint of Trebizond and a former resident of that city

REPRESENTATIVE OBVERSE LEGENDS OF THE
EMPIRE OF TREBIZOND

John I   1235–1238
(1)   (2)   (3)

```
   I    O         I              I
   Ʋ    K         W   ∴O         W    O
   Ӄ    ᚺ         Ӄ   K          Ӄ    K
   NI   N         N   ᚺ          NI   ᚺ
   ∴C∴            N   N          C*   N
                  C
```

Manuel I   1238–1263
(1)   (2)   (3)   (4)

```
   M        ᚺ∴ ∴O        ᚺ    O         ᚺ    O
   И   O    И   .K       N   ⅀K         NK   K
   Hλ  K    ∧B           I∧   N         I
   *   N                               ∧∧   N
```

George   1266–1280
(1)

```
   ⌐
   ⌐  Ᵽ
      Δ
      Π
      T
```

John II   1280–1297
(1)   (2)   (3)   (4)

```
   IW̅            IW̅   N        IW̅    N    W
   O   N         O    O        O     O    KO   II
   K   O         KO   S        KO    ✡C        O
   ᚺN            ᚺN            ᚺN              .
```

Theodora   1285
(1)

```
   θC    H
   O     KO
   ⬥     ᚺN
   W     HN
   PA
```

Alexius II 1297–1330
(1)   (2)   (3)

```
   A              A    *N            A
   ―              ―                  ∧CO   ᚺN
   Ɛ              Ɛ    K             Ɣ
   Ǝ    BN        Ǝ
                  O
```

Basil   1332-1340

(1)   (2)

$\overline{BA}$ ⊬   BA   ⊬
·

John III   1342-1344   **Michael 1344-1349**

(1)   (2)   (1)

$\overline{IW}$ O $I\overline{W}$ *   X   M

KO   OK   ⊬   MI

⊬

Alexius III   1349-1390

(1)   (2)   (3)   (4)

A   M   A   ⋀N   A   ⊬N   A

-          ～   N·   ⋀Є   B   ⋀

C   Є   Є

⋏   ⋏

KO

Manuel III   1390-1417

(1)   (2)   (3)   (4)

⊬   ⊬   ⊬   ⊬   ⊬   ⊬   A   ⊬

AO   B   AO   K   ⊬ O

⋀   B   K

Alexius IV   1417-1446

(1)   (2)   (3)

A   ⋀H   A   M   A   ⊬

⋏C   B   Є   A

⋏

who had been martyred by Diocletian in the fourth century. He is
usually depicted as a bearded, nimbate figure holding a cross in his right
hand. When the emperors changed their obverse type from standing to
mounted, they also put the good saint on horseback, a rather unusual
portrayal of an early churchman.

Reverses portraying other entities than St. Eugenius are rare. The
Virgin is shown on the scyphate silver coins of Manuel I, John the Baptist
is shown on a bronze of John II, while the emperor George put St. George
on some of his bronze issues. Various forms of the cross are common in
the bronze series but even here St. Eugenius's name frequently is placed
in the angles of the cross. The walls of the city of Trebizond and the
imperial double headed eagle are found as reverse types on certain
bronzes of Alexius III. In addition the eagle is quite common as a reverse in the anonymous series (see appendix).

Some emperors commonly placed symbols (see appendix) on their

REPRESENTATIVE REVERSE LEGENDS OF THE
EMPIRE OF TREBIZOND

General legends of the St. Eugenius type

(1)
```
  O      ∴
 Ⓐ  ϵV
 ΓI  Γϵ
  O    NI
      O
```

(2)
```
  O       ∴
 A    ϵ
 ΓI     V
      Γϵ
  O    NI
      O
```

(3)
```
  O        *
 Á    ϵV
 ΓIO *  ϵ
  \  *  N-I
         /
```

(4)
```
 Ⓐ   NI
 ϵV   O
 ΓC   S
```

(5)
```
 Ⓐ  Γϵ
 Ɛ   NI
 V    O
        C
```

(6)
```          Γϵ
 Ⓐ    N-I
 ϵVθ   O
          C
```

(7)
```
 Ⓐ   N
 ϵV
  Γ   B
```

(8)
```
 Ⓐ    Γϵ
 ϵV   N
```

(9)
```
 A    N
  V
 ϵ    .
```

(10)
```
 A    N
 ϵV
  Γ   O
```

(11)
```
 Ⓐ  и
 ϵ
  V   B
```

(12)
```
 Ⓐ   ϵV
 ΓI  ΓC
      NI
```

Special legends restricted to only one reign

(1) John the Baptist (John II)

```
 Ⓐ  ⋔
 W
 O  O
```

(2) Monogram of the Virgin (Manuel I)

```
 ⋔   ‾ϵV‾
```

APPENDIX I. The Anonymous Bronze Coinage of Trebizond.

The following are representative of the unattributed bronze coins of Trebizond. They are commonly believed to have been issued by Alexius IV or his successors.

OBVERSE | REVERSE

(1) Eagle, may be facing, to right or to left, wings spread

B . B
or
B * B

(2) Eagle as above

Cross planted on a city wall

(3) * B *

Cross with letter in each angle:
A Γ
Є И

(4) Cross potent   Cross potent

APPENDIX II. Sceptre types of Trebizond

(1) Empearled sceptre of Alexius II and Michael - ⁝̣

(2) Trident (triple headed) sceptre of Basil and Alexius III   - Ψ

(3) Triple barred sceptre of Manuel III and Alexius IV   - ⧙

APPENDIX III. Symbols found on Trebizond Coinage.

John II (obverse) - ✡
Alexius II (floral types) - Ѱ Ѱ   ↓   ⚵
Alexius III (floral types) - ⚘ Ѱ
            (sun bursts) - ✳ ✳
Manuel III and Alexius IV (floral types) - Ѱ V

coins in addition to the types and legends. John II favored a six pointed star generally below the obverse, the legend on the right; Alexius II, who struck mounted types, used various floral symbols both on the obverse and reverse below the horses. Alexius III used floral types in a similar manner and in addition frequently placed sunbursts above the obverse horse on the right. Manuel III and Alexius IV often placed small floral symbols below both obverse and reverse horses but generally these symbols are not as striking as those of the earlier rulers. Symbolism was generally restricted to the silver coinage, the bronze coins being free from these designs.

No coins have been attributed to the Emperors Alexius I, Andronicus I, II, and III, Manuel II, Irene, Anna, John IV, and David. The last two may have had some part in striking the anonymous bronze series, but this is largely conjecture.

Fig. 6. Silver asper of Alexius III of Trebizond.
Fig. 7. Silver half-asper of Alexius IV of Trebizond.

THE COINAGE OF THESSALONICA AND EPIRUS

Although their coinage is rather rare, some mention should be made of the types and inscriptions found on the coins struck by the Despotate of Epirus and the Empire of Thessalonica.

When Constantinople fell to the Crusaders in 1204, a Greek general, Michael Angelus Comnenus Ducas, retired to the hill of Epirus and established a "splinter empire" in much the same manner as Theodore Lascaris had done in western Asia Minor. Michael maintained himself and expanded his holdings against the "Latins." He was succeeded by his very capable brother Theodore Angelus who seized Thessalonica from its "Latin" ruler in 1222. Theodore then caused himself to be crowned "Emperor of the Romans" and claimed to be the legitimate successor to the old Byzantine throne. This was a rather good claim, since he was related to the old imperial family. Unfortunately for his plans, Theodore became involved with the Bulgarians and was soon captured and blinded. His brother Manuel succeeded as emperor. Eventually Theodore was released and on his return to his capital replaced Manuel with his son John Angelus. Without Theodore's strong hand at the helm, Thessalonica was unable to resist the power of the Nicaean empire and in 1243 John Ducas Vatatzes forced John Angelus to resign his title of emperor and accept the lesser rank of despot. Demetrius Angelus, John's successor as despot, was unable to hold even that title and the territories of Thessalonica were incorporated with those of Nicaea.

The coins struck by these nations are identical with those of Comnenian Byzantium and Nicaea in fabric, types, and to a great extent in inscriptions. The same reverse and obverse types are used and the average collector has a difficult time in differentiating them from the other two series. On a few coins of Thessalonica the name of the city appears in Greek which allows an accurate identification to be made. Otherwise it is almost impossible without a detailed guide. It is recommended that if the average collector obtains a coin of this period which does not easily fit into either the Byzantine or Nicaean series, he should seek the advice of an expert as to its exact attribution. The coins of Thessalonica and Epirus are rare and usually of some value.

APPENDIX IV. Chronological List of the Emperors of Trebizond

Alexius I	1204-1222*	Andronicus III	1330-1332*
Andronicus I	1222-1235*	Manuel II	1332 *
John I	1235-1238	Basil	1332-1340
Manuel I	1238-1263	Irene	1340-1341*
Andronicus II	1263-1266*	Anna	1341-1342*
George	1266-1280	John III	1342-1344
John II	1280-1297	Michael	1344-1349
Theodora	1285	Alexius III	1349-1390
Alexius II	1297-1330	Manuel III	1390-1417

Alexius IV	1417-1446
John IV	1446-1458*
David	1458-1461*

(Rulers marked * are not known to have issued coins in their own name.)

PRINCIPAL REFERENCES

ACKERMAN, J. 1834. *A Descriptive Catalogue of Rare and Unedited Roman Coins.* 2 Vols. London.

FINLAY, G. 1877. *A History of Greece.* Vol. IV. Clarendon Press, Oxford.

GIBBON, E. 1946. *The Decline and Fall of the Roman Empire,* ed. by J. B. Bury, 3 Vols. Heritage Press, New York.

GOODACRE, H. 1933. *Handbook to Coinage of the Byzantine Empire,* Part III. Isaac I to Constantine XI. Spink and Sons, London.

SABATIER, J. 1862. *Description General des Monnaies Byzantines.* 2 Vols. Paris.

VASILIEV, A. A. 1952. *History of the Byzantine Empire,* University of Wisconsin Press, Madison.

WROTH, W. 1911. *Coin of the Vandals, Ostrogoths, and Lombards, and the Empires of Thessalonica, Nicaea, and Trebizond in the British Museum.* Oxford Press, London.

PART III. BARBARIC IMITATIONS

European coinage following the collapse of the western Roman empire has always presented a confusing picture since most of the coins, whether struck by the barbarians or by the remaining eastern imperial mints, bear some allusion to the emperor on the obverse and generally follow the Roman reverse pattern. This problem is especially vexing to the Byzantine collector since he frequently encounters such imitative coins in bulk lots of Byzantine bronzes and occasionally even in lots of silver and gold. Since these imitative coinages are generally neglected by the authors of basic numismatic references, it was felt that it would be of value to include a brief discussion of them in conjunction with this series on East Roman coinage.

For the sake of brevity, only those barbarian coinages which closely resemble Byzantine issues in style and fabric or are sufficiently common to be encountered occasionally will be considered in any great detail. The rarer imitative coinages will be covered in a general manner only. The coinages of the kingdoms of the Vandals and the Ostrogoths fall into the first category while the rarer coinages, generally in gold, include the issues struck by the Visigoths in Spain, the Burgundians and Franks in Gaul, and the Lombards in Italy.

The same approach used in the two earlier East Roman papers will be followed here. Initially, in the case of the commoner issues, a brief history will be given, followed by a review of their coinage. Finally a list of representative obverse and reverse legends will be presented. The rarer issues will be covered in a less comprehensive manner.

The principal reference used for the Vandal and Ostrogoth coinages was the British Museum catalog by Warwick Wroth published in 1911, and although other references were consulted, his attributions were accepted as final. In any case of doubt the reader is advised to consult this reference.

THE VANDALS

GAISERIC (428-477) is the first Vandal king of numismatic importance. This ruler succeeded to the throne while his tribe was still in Spain and was responsible for its crossing into northern Africa. Roman Africa was easily conquered by the Vandals and by 435 even Carthage was in their hands. Gaiseric was strong enough by 455 to raid Italy and sack Rome, establishing the Vandals as the main power in the western Mediterranean area. After a long reign of 49 years, Gaiseric was succeeded by his son

HUNERIC (477-484) who continued his father's policies. Unfortunately, Huneric also initiated religious persecution of the Orthodox Christians (the Vandals were Arian Christians) which weakened the internal stability of the nation. Simultaneously the native Moors began a series of intermittent insurrections against the Vandals which continued until their overthrow.

GUNTHAMUND (484-496), a nephew of Huneric, was the third Vandal king. The new ruler was somewhat milder than his predecessors and did little to control the internal strife. At his death, his brother

TRASAMUND (496-523) was selected as king. Of all the Vandal rulers, a rather rough crowd, Trasamund is the most attractive figure from a modern viewpoint being a dashing and somewhat romantic ruler. Despite numerous campaigns, however, Trasamund was unable to control the internal rebellions although he kept the nation intact during his reign. His successor

HILDERIC (523-530), the now aged son of Huneric, was just not able to control his rebellious subjects and after an especially humiliating defeat by the Moors, the Vandal nobility deposed him in favor of

GELIMER (530-533), a nephew of Gunthamund and great-grandson of Gaiseric. Unfortunately for Gelimer, his predecessor had made an alliance with the eastern emperor, Justinian. When Justinian heard of Hilderic's deposition, he decided the time was ripe to regain Africa for the empire and sent Belisarius, his best general, to Africa with a large army on the pretext that he was coming to the aid of his ally. Gelimer rallied the Vandals but they were no match for the revitalized Romans and after several battles, the Vandal kingdom was destroyed and Gelimer was sent a prisoner to Constantinople. North Africa was again a Roman province and remained so until the Arabs conquered it in the eighth century.

Types and Inscriptions

Vandal coinage follows the Roman lead and only occasionally shows signs of independence. The only gold coins believed of Vandalic origin were struck by Gaiseric in the name of Valentinian III and by Trasamund in the name of Anastasius I. The silver coinage was more profuse and toward the end of the kingdom bore distinctive marks. Initially both Gaiseric and Huneric struck imitative siliquae in the name of Honorius. Gunthamund, however, issued siliquae in his own name and instituted its half and quarter values, each with its own distinctive marking based on one hundred bronze denari. With a few variations, these denominations were retained by all of his successors.

Gaiseric struck only imitative bronze pieces but after the fall of Carthage, a series of bronze denominational coins were issued. Those attributed to Gaiseric by Wroth have a standing Vandal soldier on the obverse with the legend KARTHAGO while a horsehead over a Roman numeral denomination served as the reverse type. Huneric changed the obverse type to a standing female personification of Carthage holding corn ears in outstretched hands and removed the horsehead from the reverse, surrounding the value mark with a heavy wreath. These distinctive coins were discontinued by their successors who substituted masses of small, crude, imitative Roman coins bearing an emperor's bust on the obverse and using typical Roman reverses including imperial monograms, large letters, walking victories, and even the "two emperors" types. The legends on both faces are usually badly blundered. The only major exception is a bronze issue of Gelimer on which he used his monogram as the reverse type and a bust of himself on the obverse. These small bronzes are attributed to emperors from Honorius to Justinian when the legend is sufficiently legible to make such distinction.

Fig. 1. Bronze 21 nummi piece of Gaiseric. It should be noted that the "nummi" of the Vandals were not strictly imitative of the Byzantine "nummia" since they were instituted almost 50 years prior to the reforms of Anastasius. (ANS Collection).

Fig. 2. Bronze 42 nummi piece of Huneric. (ANS Collection)

Fig. 3. Silver "100 denari" coin of Gunthamund. Note how closely this piece resembles the contemporary Roman siliqua. (ANS Collection)

REPRESENTATIVE VANDALIC OBVERSE LEGENDS

Gaiseric (bronze only)
1. KARTHAÇO
Gunthamund (silver only)
1. DN REX GVNTHAMVND
Trasamund (silver only)
1. DN RǪ THSAMVNDS
Hilderic (silver only)
1. DN HILDIRIX REX
Gelimer
1. ÇEIL (bronze only)
2. DN REX ÇEILAMIR (silver only)

REPRESENTATIVE VANDALIC REVERSE LEGENDS

Gaiseric
1.
   X‖II‖ (42 nummi)
2.
   XXI (21 nummi)
3.
   XII (12 nummi)

Huneric
1.
   N X̄·‖II‖ (42 nummi)
2.
   N X̄X̄ I (21 nummi)
3.
   N̄ X̄II (12 nummi)
4. N̄
   IIII (4 nummi)

Gunthamund (silver only)

1.
  D•N
(100 denari)

2.
  D•N
(50 denari)

3.
  D•N (25 denari)
  XXV

Trasamund (silver only)
1.
  D•N (50 denari)

Hilderic (silver only)
1. FELIX CARTA
(50 denari)
2. XXV
(25 denari)

Gelimer
1. D•N (50 denari)

2. (monogram of Gelimer)

REPRESENTATIVE TYPES AND LEGENDS FOUND ON VANDALIC SMALL BRONZE COINS

Obverse types and legends: The obverse of these small coins, weighing rarely over 20 grains and not usually over 0.5 inches in diameter, is generally occupied by a bust right, wearing diadem and drapery, although a cuirass is sometimes worn. A legend, usually blundered, is present, attributing these issues all the way from Honorius to Justinian I. Examples of these legends are:

1. IVS NIAN (bust Justinian I right)
2. DNVA   INIA (bust Valentinian III right)
3. DOMINO NOSTRO (unknown emperor facing right)
4. HONORI (bust Honorius right)

Reverse types and legends: Many varied reverse types are found in this series. Victory, standing or walking right or left is common. The "Roma seated" reverse so popular in the fourth century is frequently seen, and the standing emperor reverses are all present. The depicted figures are grotesque and sometimes merely implied. Blundered forms of the VICTORIA AVGGG, VICTORIA AVGVSTORVM, SALVS REIPVBLICAE, and even PAX AVG, legends are seen with these types. Two somewhat more distinctive reverse series found in this group of coins are (1) the imperial monograms of the Byzantine type and (2) letter reverses. Examples of these are as follows:

Monograms of Byzantine emperors

Theodosius II

Marcian

Leo I

Zeno

Anastasius I

Justinian I

Letter reverse types

THE OSTROGOTHS

When compared to the Vandals the Ostrogoths were a comparatively civilized people having been in contact with the Romans for centuries. As early as the third and fourth centuries many of them had served with the Roman armies, especially under Theodosius I, and a few had even attained high place in the Roman government. However, a series of unfortunate episodes drove them into warfare against the Romans and by the end of the fifth century they had invaded deep into the Balkan peninsula. The emperor Zeno, after the Herulian chief, Odovacer, had deposed Romulus Augustulus, hit upon the idea of using barbarian to destroy barbarian, and formally gave

THEODORIC (493-526), the young king of the Ostrogoths, permission to reconquer Italy for the empire. Theodoric agreed and marched the Ostrogoths en masse into Italy eventually deposing Odovacer. Then, as the emperor's agent, he organized his conquest into a Gothic kingdom theoretically under the supreme jurisdiction of Constantinople. Italy under Theodoric was a bright spot during this somewhat dismal period, and was one of the few places where commerce and education were encouraged. Unfortunately, when he died he was succeeded by his 10-year-old grandson

ATHALARIC (526-534) under the regency of AMALASUNTHA, his daughter. Amalasuntha was very partial to things Roman and brought her son up in what the more primitive Goths considered to be an effeminate manner. Finally, the Gothic nobility forced Amalasuntha to retire as regent and allowed the young king to shift for himself. It was an unwise step for Athalaric fell into evil ways and soon died from, as many believe, overindulgence. Amalasuntha was again elevated to power as queen but since the Goths wished to have a male ruler, she was encouraged to marry. As her new consort, she selected

THEODAHAD (534-536), a distant relative. Theodahad, although a scholar and a man of apparent character, turned out to be a rather weak and vicious individual. Within a very short time he murdered his bride and seized sole power. As had previously happened in Africa, Justinian had made a treaty with Amalasuntha some years earlier and when he heard of her death, he immediately threatened to invade Italy. Theodahad was terrified and tried to pacify the emperor but in doing so he antagonized his own Goths and was deposed. The Goths then elected as king one of the leading generals

WITIGES (536-540). Shortly after his accession, Witiges forced the young daughter of Amalasuntha and sister of Athalaric, MATASUNTHA, to marry him to give greater validity to his claim to the Ostrogothic throne. Unfortunately for the new king, Justinian had already decided

Fig. 4. Solidus struck by Theodoric in the name of Anastasius I. Note the monogram of Theodoric in the left reverse field. (ANS Collection)

Fig. 5. Small bronze 5 nummia piece of Theodoric. (ANS Collection)

Fig. 6. Silver quarter-siliqua of Theodoric. (ANS Collection)

Fig. 7. Bronze 10 nummia piece of Athalaric. Note the small letters "SC" on either side of the standing king on the reverse as well as the denomination mark, X.

Fig. 8. Silver quarter-siliqua of Theodahad.

Fig. 9. Quarter-siliqua of Baudila struck in the name of Anastasius rather than in the name of his contemporary, Justinian I. (ANS Collection)

Fig. 10. Bronze 40 nummia "quasi-autonomous" coin of Rome.

NON-BYZANTINE OBVERSE OSTROGOTHIC LEGENDS

Athalaric
  1. INVICTA ROMA (with bust of Roma)
Theodahad
  1. DN THEODAHATVS (bronze only)
Baudilia (silver and bronze)
  1. DN BADVILA RIX
  2. DN BADVELA REX

REPRESENTATIVE REVERSE TYPES AND LEGENDS
OF THE OSTROGOTHS

Theodoric
  1. Monograms

    a.   b.

    (silver reverse   (used in reverse field
       type)   of gold coins)

  2. Denominational reverses for 5 nummia:

    a. Є   b. V

Athalaric
  1. Monogram (used on ½ siliqua and on bronzes)

    D [monogram] N

  2. Inscription in wreath :   D N
    (used on ¼ siliqua and   A T H A
    on bronze issues)   L A R I
                      C V S

  3. Denominational reverses:

    a. X (10 nummia)   b. Є or V
                          (5 nummia)

  4. DN ATHALARICVS around a standing figure of
the king is found on some 10 nummia pieces.

Theodahad
  1. Monograms (used on ½ siliqua and bronzes)

    a.   b.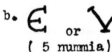

  2. Inscription in wreath :   D N
    (used on ¼ siliqua   THEODA
    and on bronze issues)   HATHVS
                           REX

Theodahad (continued)
3. Denominational reverses

a. (10 nummia) b. (5 nummia)

4. VICTORIA PRINCIPVM (Victory standing rt)

Witiges
1. Inscription in wreath :   DN
   (used on ½ siliqua and   VVIT
   on 10 nummia bronze   IGES
   with X in field)   REX
2. This monogram of Theodoric was used on his
½.siliqua:

Matasuntha (grand-daughter of Theodoric and wife
of Witiges)
1. Monogram used on ½, ¼ siliqua
                and on bronzes :

Baudila
1. Monogram used on bronzes:

                                       DN
2. Inscription in wreath :   BADV
   (used on ½ and ¼   ILA
        siliqua)   REX
3.
   FLOREAS SEMPER (legend on 10 nummia piece, X
in field, with figure of Baudila standing right)
Theia   D N
1. Inscription in wreath :   THE
                                       I A
                                       REX

---

to regain Italy for the empire and Belisarius was sent there with a large army. Witiges fought well but was no match for Belisarius and after four years the principal cities of Italy were in his hands and Witiges himself was a prisoner. In their hour of defeat, the Goths elected

ILDIBAD (540-541), the son of the king of the Visigoths, their ruler. Ildibad was able to inflict one defeat on the imperialists, as the Romans were called, but died suddenly before much could be accomplished. Then a new king

ERARIC (541) was elected but assassinated shortly after his succession. The Goths then chose a nephew of Ildibad

BAUDILA (541-552) king. Baudila, or as he is sometimes called, Totila, was a brilliant general and an extremely good administrator. His character was one of the finest of that period and he has been compared with the best of the Roman emperors. Baudila was able to hold his own against the imperialists and even recaptured Rome. He ruled for 11 years but eventually a new army was sent to Italy from Constantinople under Narses, Justinian's other fine general, and in the new struggle Baudila was killed. Although their cause now appeared hopeless, the Goths chose

THEIA (552-553), one of Baudila's generals, for their new king. Theia was killed shortly afterwards in a pitched battle and the Goths surrendered. They were permitted to march north over the Alps and out of history, and Italy, as well as Africa, was again a Roman province.

Types and Inscriptions

Ostrogothic coinage, like that of the Vandals, follows the Roman pattern quite closely. None of the kings coined gold in his own name but Theodoric struck both solidi and tremisses in the name of Anastasius and Justin I, Athalaric in the name of Justin I and Justinian I, Theodahad and Witiges in the name of Justinian I, while Baudila and Theia, at war against Justinian, used Anastasius on their gold coinages.

Ostrogothic silver coinage is another matter. The usual procedure was to place the emperor's bust, usually to the right, on the obverse while the reverse was occupied by either the Ostrogothic king's full name or monogram, the whole surrounded by a wreath. The siliqua, copied from the Romans, was struck customarily in the half and quarter denomi-

Quasi-Autonomous Bronze Coins
of Rome and Ravenna

Rome

Obverses

1. IMP ZENO SEMPERA (bust of Zeno rt)
2. INVICTA (IMVICTA, IИVICTΛ) ROMA (bust of Roma right)

Reverses

1. XL or ⅃X (40 nummia)   2. XX or .X.X. (20 nummia)

Ravenna

Obverse: FELIX RAVENNA (bust of Ravenna right)

Reverses:

1. R V (Victory advancing left)   2. RE or RE (monogram of city)

3. All have ✗ in field. (10 nummia)

nations. The emperor occupying the obverse of the Gothic coinage is usually the king's contemporary at Constantinople with the exception of Baudila and Theia, who, as with their gold, used Anastasius except in a few rare instances.

The Ostrogothic bronze issues are similar to the silver ones bearing the emperor's head on the obverse with the reverse occupied with either the king's name, his monogram, a denominational mark showing the value in nummi, or as in one of Theodahad's issues, a standing victory. The only kings who actually depicted themselves on the obverses were Theodahad and Baudila.

Athalaric struck some 10 nummia pieces showing himself standing as a reverse type. During the reigns of Theodoric and Athalaric, the cities of Rome and Ravenna struck a series of quasi-autonomous bronze coins in the denominations of forty (XL), twenty (XX), and ten (X) nummia. The coins struck at Rome commonly had a helmeted bust of Roma as the obverse type with the legend IMVICTA ROMA, and had as reverse types, in addition to the mark of value, either an eagle with spread wings, two eagles by a fig tree, or the old Roman wolf and twins. The Ravenna issues used a bust of Ravenna wearing a mural crown and the legend FELIX RAVENNA on the obverse and had either a Victory, the wolf and twins, or the city monogram on the reverse. A large bronze coin bearing the bust of Zeno on the obverse and a Victory on the reverse believed issued by Odovacer prior to the Ostrogothic invasion is usually included in this quasi-autonomous series.

It is interesting to note that on a few of the bronze coins struck by the Ostrogoths, the old Roman notation SC (Senatus Consulto) appears for the last time. When present, it is found on the reverse and is never especially prominent.

PART III. BARBARIC IMITATIONS

THE LOMBARD KINGDOM AND THE DUCHY OF BENEVENTO

The Italy that Justinian added to his empire was not the Italy of the old Roman days. The continual barbarian invasions followed by the long Gothic war had devastated the countryside and depleted the population. There were large tracts completely uninhabited and formerly prosperous cities had degenerated into armed camps. It was also unfortunate that although Justinian eagerly sought new territories, he did little to rehabilitate them after they were conquered, and other than placing garrisons in the larger towns did nothing to insure the permanency of his new province. Such a land, poorly garrisoned, and almost uninhabited was naturally inviting to peoples seeking a new home and after a few years the Byzantine empire was destined to lose most of the peninsula.

In 568, the Lombards under their chief Alboin crossed the Alps and descended into the Italian plains. The feeble Byzantine garrisons were at best able to hold only the major towns and soon all that was left of Byzantine Italy was a strip across the middle from Ravenna to Rome and part of the boot. Even this remaining territory was subject to constant raids and by the late eighth century only a few parts of southern Italy remained in the emperor's hands.

The coinage of the Lombards was completely imitative of Byzantine issues until the reign of Cunincpert in 688, when an independent coinage was first produced. Prior to this, the coins, all gold tremisses, were very crude copies of current Byzantine strikings. Often they were quite broad and thin, resembling the bracteates of the later middle ages. They were, however, regardless of diameter, tremisses by weight. The only clue as to the issuing king prior to Cunincpert is to decipher the obverse legend and match the emperor named against his contempory Lombard king. Even this is not foolproof since the kings were not averse to using emperors long dead on their coins. Another difficulty encountered is that the legends are badly bungled and only occasionally will there be enough to make an intelligible name. The Lombards favored the cross on three steps (VICTORIA AVGGG) reverse although they did use a walking Victory in a few cases.

After Cunincpert, the Lombards adopted a nationalistic coinage with the king's name in the obverse legend. Of course, the bust used to depict the king is the same one that had formerly depicted the emperor but since the name is given in the legend, it is easy to distinguish these later issues from the imitative earlier ones. They also adopted new reverse types, the most popular being St. Michael. By the late eighth century the Lombard coinage had become quite characteristic and it is not easily mistaken for that struck at Constantinople.

The independent duchy of Beneventum was one of four established in Italy during the Lombard wars, but it was the only one that struck its own coins. The dukes (and later princes) of Beneventum copied the Byzantine gold coinage quite closely until the reign of Grimoald III. This ruler, no doubt inspired by the elevation of his nation to the rank of principality, struck a new distinctive coinage in both gold and silver using the prince's bust as the obverse type and monograms and St. Michael in place of the Byzantine cross as reverse types.

Prior to Grimoald's reform, the Beneventum issues were imitative of Byzantine solidi and tremisses, mainly those of Justinian II. However, in a number of cases these coins can be differentiated from those of the empire by the fact that the dukes often placed a distinguishing mark in the reverse field, usually to the left of the cross. Occasionally two letters may be used, one on each side of the cross.

It is interesting to note that both the Lombard kings and the ruler of Beneventum faithfully copied the Byzantine mint mark CONOB. Often it's the only legend on the coin that is not blundered beyond all recognition. (Originally the CON was believed to have referred to Constantinople and the OB an abbreviation for "obryzum" or "pure gold.")

IMITATIVE COINAGES IN SPAIN AND GAUL

Spain and Gaul were two of the first imperial provinces to feel the effects of the collapse of the old Rhine-Danube barrier in the fifth century. As early as the middle of the fourth century, the Franks were hammering at the Rhine frontier and only the brilliant campaigns of the emperor Julian prevent them from seizing Gaul at that time. In the east, the Visigoths were actually permitted to cross the Danube and settle on the frontier with the idea of obtaining their aid in stemming other tribes trying to break into the empire. Unfortunately, the greed of the Roman governors forced the Visigoths into revolt and the Roman emperor Valens was killed and his army destroyed by them at Hadrianople.

Theodosius I managed to control the Goths but at his death, they again went into revolt and drove deep into the Balkan peninsula, seizing Athens. Then under their great chief Alaric I, they proceeded to Italy and sacked Rome. Finally they moved west through southern Gaul and settled in Spain, incidentally driving the Vandals, who had previously invaded Spain, into Africa. About the same time, the Franks were able to breech the Rhine barrier and enter Gaul settling in the northern part of the country while another barbarian tribe, the Burgundians, crossed and settled in southeastern Gaul. Although the imperial armies held portions of these former provinces for a while, by the end of the reign of Honorius they had lost practically all of them.

The Visigoths, in contrast to the semi-nationalistic practice later adopted by the Ostrogoths of placing their king's name on the reverse of their coins, struck a strictly imitative coinage until late in the sixth century when king Leovigild (573-586) abandoned the imperial obverse

Obverse legends: As noted in the text, these were merely badly blundered Byzantine legends from Justinian I to after Constantine III.

Some examples:
1. ︎ИNNSTAIVIAC (Justinian I)
2. OIIVST NVS PPAII (Justin II)
3. DNⲘAVRC TIPA (Maurice Tiberius)
4. DN HIRACLVIPAVG (Heraclius)
5. VITONIA AVTINSVI (Constantine III ?)

Reverse legends: Blundered versions of the VICTORIA AVGGG and VICTORIA AVGVSTORVM legends were most popular. Some examples:
1. ICTORIA AVIVITI   3. VICTORIA AVIVITORVN
2. VIII ︎ⲦOTVIVITO   4. IOVIVVIO

The mint mark, CONOB, was also usually copied, and blundered. Examples:
1. INOB   2. COIIOR   3. CONOR   4. ᴐOⲘOI

COINAGE OF THE DUKES OF THE INDEPENDENT LOMBARD DUCHY OF BENEVENTUM

Obverse legends: The usual type was the facing bust of Justinian II. The legends were often blundered: Some examples:
1. DN IꙨST INIANVS PPꞒA 3. DⲘ IVNPP
2. DN IV⁓TINIVN   4. DNI INVSPP

The standard reverse was the cross potent on three steps with the VICTORIA AVGGG or VICTORIA AVGVSTORVM legend. Some blundered examples:
1. VICTOR AVGV   3. VICT VꝖTO
2. VICTO RIVVꝖ   4. VICTRꝺ ꝖGVSTV

The rulers of Beneventum placed the following letters in the reverse field to indicate the issuing authority for the coin:

Romoald II	Ɍ	Liutprand (with Scauniperga)	S L	Arichis II A
Gregorius	Ꝿ			
Gisulf	Ɍ Ꝿ	Liutprand (alone)	L	

and used his own bust and titles on his issues. Although imitative tremisses of Valentinian III have been found in Spain, these are now believed issues of the Suevi, another barbarian tribe which invaded Spain prior to the Visigoths, and the first imitative coins definitely attributed to the Visigothic kings are tremisses struck in the name of Anastasius I (491-518). These coins, and the imitative Visigothic pieces struck in the names of his three successors, are quite characteristic when compared with the real Byzantine coins of these emperors.

The legends on Visigothic coins are frequently clumsily copied but usually not as severely as they are by the Lombard kings. One of the most common errors was reversing letters like R, C, or S or copying them upside down. Customarily, the bust of the emperor, usually to the right, occupied the obverse, while a Victory, walking to the right and bearing the palm, was the standard reverse type. The Victory used by the Visigoths is very characteristic and if once seen can usually be identified again without difficulty. As one expert states, it resembles an upright grasshopper more than a winged human. Needless to say, the CONOB mint mark was faithfully copied.

Generally speaking, it is difficult to attribute any particular coin to an exact king in most cases. The best that can be done is to match the emperor on the obverse with the contemporary Visigothic rulers. This is not always too successful since Anastasius had four Visigothic counterparts, Euric, Alaric II, Gesalic, and Amalaric. The Visigothic coins of Justin I can be assigned more accurately since the reign of Amalaric (511-531) encompassed the entire reign of Justin. Also, on some of his coins, the Goth placed his monogram on the reverse definitely assigning the coins to his reign. The imitative coins of Justinian I are hard to attribute since no less than five Visigothic kings ruled in Spain during his long reign. The imitative tremisses of Justin II are the last struck by the Visigoths and are clearly inferior to those previously issued. The legends are more frequently erroneous and the art work quite inferior. Leovigild discontinued these imitative issues on his accession and struck coins bearing his own bust and titles. He did not however, abandon the reverse types and the Victory. Later the Byzantine cross on steps reverse was used by many of the Visigothic kings. After Leovigild's reign, the Visigothic coinage is no longer imitative and is easily distinguished from the contemporary Byzantine issues.

Visigothic coins are quite rare and it is doubtful if the average collector will ever see much less own one. A word of warning in this regard is probably indicated here. The notorious forger, Karl Becker, struck a number of Visigothic forgeries, mostly of the kings subsequent to Leovigild. These are sometimes offered for sale to the unwary as real Visigothic issues. The average collector should beware of such offers especially if he is offered a "denarius." The Visigoths struck essentially nothing but gold tremisses and a silver coin is automatically suspect.

The coinages of the Franks and Burgundians follow the Visigothic pattern, first being imitative of the Roman and later developing into a nationalistic form. The first Frankish kings, the Merovingians, copied the imperial issues but very early, in the reign of Theodebert I (534-547) the king substituted his name and titles for the emperor's on the obverse. By the reign of Clovis II, not only was the king's name listed but those of the moneyers as well. Often the king's name would be omitted and that of the town where the coin was struck inserted.

After 600 the supply of gold gradually was reduced and finally in 752, Pepin I, one of the early Carolingian kings, demonetized the gold coinage and issued a "novus denarius" in silver. The Franks originally struck large gold solidi but as the gold shortage developed, they too adopted the tremissis as the standard denomination. As late as the seventh century, however, Massila (Marseilles) in southern Gaul issued "solidi" in the name of Heraclius with a bungled VICTORIA AVGV-STORVM reverse and with the initials "M A" in the field to show the place of issue.

The Burgundian coinage followed the pattern set by the Franks and need not be discussed at any length. A good example of their coinage is found in a very crude imitative solidus of Anastasius struck by their greatest king, Gondebald (473-516), in which a retrograde monogrammed BVR was placed in the reverse field to denote its source. The Burgundian kingdom was conquered in 534 by the Franks under Clotair and its existence as a separate nation ceased.

Collectors interested in additional study of these interesting coinages are referred to the excellent references by Engel and Surrure, the *Traite de Numismatique,* published in several volumes between 1891 and 1905 at Paris, for the Merovingian issues and to both Heiss and Mateo y Llopis for a wealth of information on the Visigothic series. The excellent text by George Miles published by the American Numismatic Society on Visigothic coinage from Leovigild to Achila II is very complete and has the additional virtue of still being in print. As is so common with all standard numismatic references, the others are somewhat difficult to obtain.

Thus far, one particular form of barbaric imitative coinage, the so-called "barbarous radiates," has not been considered since they are not strictly Byzantine but rather crude copies of the Roman antoniniani of the 3rd century, especially those struck by the rulers of the "Gallic Empire" founded by Postumus in the reign of Gallienus. Some mention of these coins, however, might be of value, though, since it will give the reader some basis for comparison between barbarous radiates and the imitative coinages of the later Roman and Byzantine bronze coins such as the Vandalic small bronze series.

The barbarous radiates were struck principally in northern Europe and were especially popular in Britain. The obverse of these coins characteristically bears a spike crowned bust, usually to the right, but often it is so degenerated that only a shadow of the original design is left. When recognizable, the emperors mostly commonly depicted are the Tetrici, Claudius II, and Victorinus. Although other emperors are occasionally found, their busts are rare. The reverse usually bears one of the standard Roman personifications commonly found on antoniniani, the female ones being more common than the male ones. Pax is the commonest followed by Fides, Fortuna, Hilaritas, Salus, and Virtus in that order. Other personifications are known but are rare in the barbarous radiate series. It is believed that these coins were struck up until the 7th century becoming cruder and less recognizable with the succeeding years.

For those interested in additional information on barbarous radiates no better references can be found than Philip Hill's A.N.S. Monograph (no. 112) on barbarous radiates published in 1949. Another shorter article by the same author may be found in the appendix of the late Gilbert Askew's *"Coinage of Roman Britain"* published in 1951 by B. A. Seaby, London.

It is very difficult to do justice to such a large subject as imitative Byzantine coinages in such a short paper. However, if this article does nothing more than make the average collector aware that such coins exist, it will be well worth the time and effort required for its preparation.

Fig. 11. Imitative Lombard tremissis of Heraclius. Note the badly blundered legends, the mint mark, CONOB, being the only intact one present.

Fig. 12. Imitative solidus of Justinian II struck by Gisulf II, Duke of Beneventum, with distinguishing initials in the reverse field on either side of the cross potent. (ANS Collection)

Fig. 13. Imitative Visigothic tremissis struck by Amalaric. This variation of the cross reverse was quite popular with the Visigoths and was also used by the Suevi on their imitative coins of Valentinian III. (ANS Collection)

Chronological list of the kings of Lombardy from Alboin to the death of Cunincpert.

Alboin	568-572 (reign in Italy)
Cleph	572-574
Interregnum	574-584
Authari	584-590
Agilulf	590-615
Adalwald	615-624
Ariwald	624-636
Rothari	636-652
Rodwald	652
Aripert	653-661
Perctarit and Godepert	661-662
Grimwald	662-671
Perctarit (2nd reign)	672-688
Cunincpert	688-700

Chronological list of the Dukes of Beneventum to the death of Grimoald III.

Zotto	571-591
Arichis I	591-641
Aio	641-642
Radoald	642-647
Grimoald I (king of Lombardy, 662-671)	647-662
Romoald I	671-687
Grimoald II	687-689
Gisulf	689-706
Romoald II	706-731
Audelais	731-732
Gregorius	732-739
Gottschalk	739-742
Gisulf II	742-751 (Married Scauniperga)
Liutprand	751-758
Arichis II	758-787 (Became Prince in 774)
Grimoald III	788-806

Chronological list of the kings of the Suevi to 585

Hermeneric	409-438
Richila	438-448
Richiaric	448-456
Fratan	457
Masdran	457-460
Rechimund	457-465
Framaric	460-463
Remismund, unknown	465-468
Carriaric	550-559
Theodomir	559-569
Ariomir	561
Miron	569-582
Eboric	582-583
Audica	583-585

Chronological list of the kings of the Visigoths to the death of Leovigild

		Place of residence
Atanaric	369-382	
Alaric I	382-412	
Ataulf	412-415	Barcelona
Sigeric	415	Barcelona
Walia	415-419	Toulouse
Teodored I	419-451	Toulouse
Tursimund	451-453	Toulouse
Teodoric	453-466	Toulouse
Euric	466-484	Toulouse and Burgos
Alaric II	484-507	Toulouse
Gesaleic	507-511	Toulouse
Amalaric	511-531	Narbonne
Theudis	531-548	Barcelona
Teudisel	548-549	Barcelona
Agila	549-554	Merida
Athanagild	554-567	Toledo
Liuva	567-573	Narbonne
Leovigild	573-586	Toledo

Chronological list of the kings of Burgundy to 534

Gondowic	452-473	
Gondebaud	473-516	(at Lyons)
Godegisel	473-500	(at Besancon)
Chilperic	473-486	(at Geneva)
Gondomar	473-486	(at Vienna)
Sigismund	516-524	
Gondomar II	524-534	

Chronological list of the kings of the Merovingian Franks

Childeric 458-481
Clovis 481-511   (at his death kingdom was
   In Austrasia   divided among his sons)
Theodoric I 511-534
Theodebert I 534-547
Theodebald I 547-555
Clotair I 558-561
Seigbert I 561-575
Childebert II 575-596
Theodebert II 596-612
Clotair II 613-622
Dagobert I 622-638
Seigbert II 638-656
Childeric II 657-673
Dagobert II 673-678
Theodoric III 679-691
Chilperic II 715-720
Childeric III 743-752
   At Soissons
Clotair I 511-561   (sole king of the Franks,
                                        558-561)
Chilperic I 561-584
Clotair II 584-628
Dagobert I 628-638
   In Neustria
Clovis II 638-656
Clotair III 656-670
Theodoric III 670   (1st reign)
Childeric II 670-673
Theodoric III 673-691   (2nd reign)
Clovis III 691-695
Childebert III 695-711
Dagobert III 711-715
Chilperic II 715-720
Theodoric IV 720-737
   At Orleans
Clodomer 511-524
Theodoric II 596-613
   At Orleans and in Burgundy
Gontran 561-592
   At Paris
Childebert I 511-538
Caribert I 561-567
   In Aquitaine
Caribert II 628-636

A chronological list of the Frankish kings is confusing and difficult to follow since it was their custom to divide a kingdom between all of the king's sons at his death. Thus often the same king will appear as ruler of each of the several divisions of the Frank nation as he gradually conquered his brothers' lands or inherited them by other means. This is easily seen in the division of the unified kingdom of Clovis between his four sons (Theodoric, Clodomer, Childebert, and Clotair) at his death. By 558, Clotair had reunited the nation but again at his death in 561, the kingdom was divided between his four sons Caribert, Gontran, Chilperic, and Siegbert.

The preceding list of barbarian kings was included to give the reader a table by which he can compare the emperor depicted on his imitative Byzantine coins with the various contemporary barbarian kings. Since the Vandals and Ostrogoths were covered in the text, their rulers have not been listed. These lists are based on information from Wroth, Sergeant, Mateo y LLopis, Bradley, and the *Encyclopedia Britannica*. It should be remembered that very often even the authorities do not agree as to the exact spelling of the barbarian names or the precise dates of reign. In such cases, the dates or the spelling favored by the majority have been used.

PRINCIPLE REFERENCES

ACKERMAN, J. *A Descriptive Catalogue of Rare and Unedited Roman Coins.* 2 vols., London, 1834.

BRADLEY, H. *The Goths.* G. P. Putnam, London, 1899.

GIBBON, E. *The Decline and Fall of the Roman Empire,* edited by J. B. BURY. Heritage Press, New York, 1946.

HEISS, A. *Description Generale des Monnaies des Rois Wisigoths D'Espagne.* L'Imprimerie Nationale, Paris, 1872.

LANE-POOLE, S. *Coins and Medals.* Elliot Stock, London, 1892.

MATEO Y LLOPIS, F. *Catalogo de las Monedas Previsigodas y Visigodas Gabinete Numismatico del Museo Arqueologico Nacional.* Madrid, 1936.

MILES, G. *The Coinage of the Visigoths of Spain, Leovigild to Achila II.* American Numismatic Society, New York, 1952.

MATTINGLY, H. *A Guide to the Exhibition of Roman Coins in the British Museum.* Oxford Press, London, 1927.

OMAN, C. *The Byzantine Empire.* G. P. Putnam, London, 1898.

SABATIER, J. *Description General des Monnaies Byzantines.* 2 vol., Paris, 1862.

SERGEANT, L. *The Franks.* T. Fisher Unwin, London, 1898.

THOMSEN, C. J. *Description des Monnaies du Moyen Age.* Copenhagen, 1873.

WROTH, W. *Coins of the Vandals, Ostrogoths, and the Lombards, and the Empires of Thessalonica, Nicaea, and Trebizond in the British Museum.* Oxford Press, London, 1911.

PART IV. CONCLUSION

Moslem-Byzantine Coinage

ALTHOUGH oriental and not Byzantine, the Arab imitative coinages of the seventh century are of some interest to the East Roman collector since it is entirely possible these coins might be encountered from time to time. Because of this, the collector should be able to recognize them for what they are since they are often of some value.

When the Arab hordes swept across the near east early in the seventh century, the inhabitants were still essentially an uncultured people. For the first time in Arab history the invaders found themselves faced with the problem of governing large populated areas possessing a complicated commercial life. The simple village economy that had sufficed for the Arab tribes before was completely unable to handle this new problem. As a consequence, the Arabs were forced to adopt many of the economic forms of the conquered territories, among them money.

Generally, the Arabians merely copied the coins of their victims, using the Byzantine gold and bronze and the Sassanian Persian silver coins for their models. These early Arab imitations can usually be distinguished from their true counterparts by the inclusion of Arabic legends and by minor modifications in the designs. The imitations in bronze, the commonest of the Byzantine types, are classically copies of the Heraclian coinage. Two coins clearly illustrate the point. Fig. 1, from the A.N.S. collection, is an Arab-Byzantine bronze based on a 40 nummia piece of Heraclius. The obverse is occupied with a standing figure of the emperor (some writers prefer to call him the "Caliph" in these cases) holding the traditional long sceptre. The reverse contains the standard block "M" denominational mark. The Arabic legends indicate that this coin was struck at Damascus. Figure 2, also from the A.N.S. collection, shows a typical "three standing Augusti" Heraclian coin but the presence of Arabic legends indicate that it, too, is of Moslem origin. The block "M" again appears as the reverse type and the legends show that this particular coin was struck at Tiberias in Syria.

Finally in 695, the Omayyad Caliph Abd-al-Malik (685-705) ordered the striking of a nationalistic coinage and discontinued the Byzantine and Persian imitations. The new coins differ completely from the old in that all figures are replaced by Kufic legends on both obverse and reverse. Although there is some question in this regard, no nationalistic Arab coins dated prior to the year 76 A.H. have been found to date so Abd-al-Malik can be considered the father of Arab coinage.

Later during the Seljouk Turk domination of Asia Minor, other imitative Byzantine coins were issued bearing typical Byzantine types. The Virgin crowning the emperor was popular and the seated figure of Christ was actually used. Again, Turkish legends show the true origin of the coin. These coins are not particularly common and the average collector will seldom meet them. For additional information, the reader is referred to the *Catalogue of Oriental Coins in the British Museum, the Catalogue of Oriental Coins in the Royal Museum in Berlin,* and Marsden's *Numismata Orientalia* (London, 1823).

Condition

Although some note was made earlier on the miserable condition of the average Byzantine coin, especially the bronzes, some further comment would probably be of value. For some reason, collectors always compare the stylized and often grotesque East Roman coins with the excellent portrait coins of the early Roman empire or with the equally artistic coins of the Renaissance. This is really quite unfair and to obtain a real picture of Byzantine coinage it is necessary to compare these coins with their contemporaries from western Europe. When a coin of, say, Constantine III, is placed along aside of a sesterius of Nero, it does indeed appear to be a miserable example of numismatic art. However, when this same coin is compared to a Lombard or Visigothic tremissis, or to a Merovingian denier, its artistic superiority becomes apparent.

In the classification of condition in Byzantine coins, the standard gradings of "vf" down to "poor" are not quite valid since the average Byzantine bronze rarely rates above "good" and probably is not even entitled to this low classification. Because of this, the author, in the classification of his own Byzantine coins, has adopted another system of grading which might be of interest to other collectors since it reflects more correctly the real status of any particular coin, both as regards condition, and what is more important, rarity. The lowest grade is *unidentifiable*, (U), and is self-explanatory. The next higher grade is *acceptable* (A) and corresponds to the standard condition grades of "poor" and "fair" and to "common" in the rarity scale. *Desirable* (D) is above *acceptable* corresponding to "good" and "very good" and to "scarce." *Very desirable* (VD) corresponds to "fine" and to the lower degrees of rarity, while *extremely desirable* (ED) is used to denote the ultimate in both condition and rarity. Thus using this system, it is possible to have a common bronze coin of Justinian I in fine condition rated as *very desirable* and a "poor" coin of Tiberius III of some rarity given the same or even a higher classification.

The following illustrations might help to illustrate these points. Figures 3 and 4 (obverses of solidi of Constantine III and Constantine IV) show the condition of the average gold Byzantine coin. In most cases, gold follows most closely the standard classifications since coins that were not choice were melted down. Figure 5 (a miliaresion of Constantine VII and Romanus 11) shows a "very fine" silver coin classed as "ED." This same coin in "very good" condition would still be *extremely desirable* since it is rare and in demand as one of the few coins bearing the name of Romanus II.

The bronze coins however, show the weakness of the standard rating scale. Figure 6, a 40 nummia piece of Justin I, is typical. The legend is not complete, the bust and denomination mark are worn, and the style is crude and heavy. To the average collector, it is obviously a "junk box" candidate. Actually, however, this coin is not bad at all and can safely be classed as *acceptable*. Figure 7, a 40 nummia piece of Tiberius II, in spite of its apparent "good" to "very good" condition is almost *very desirable*. Its mint mark (CONB — Constantinople) and regal year (uI — 7 or 580/1 AD)[1] are sharp and easily read and the obverse legend can almost be read in its entirety. Figure 8, a 40 nummia piece of Heraclius, a "fair" coin at the best according to the standard rules, is really *very desirable* because of its rarity. This is because the three figures standing on the obverse depict (from right to left) Martina, the second wife of Heraclius,

---

1. The figure "u" in this case stands for the numeral "6" and dates the coin as being struck seven years after Tiberius had been admitted to the government by Justin II and not seven years after the death of Justin. If the top of the "u" had been open rather than almost closed, it would have represented the numeral "5."

Figs. 1-2. Arab-Byzantine. Fig. 3. Constantine III solidus, obv. Fig. 4. Constantine IV solidus, obv. Fig. 5. Miliaresion of Constantine VII and Romanus II. Fig. 6. 40 nummia of Justin I. Fig. 7. Bronze of Tiberius II. Fig. 8. Bronze of Heraclius. Fig. 9. Bronze of Constantine III. Fig. 10. Bronze of Constantine X.

then the emperor, and finally his eldest son, Heraclius Constantine. The presence of Martina enhances the value of the coin greatly.

Figure 9 is a 40 nummia piece of Constantine III, "very good" at the best, which again is *very desirable*. Note the grotesque little figure which is typical of the coins of this period. Incidently, Byzantine coins with the "script" 40 nummia mark "m," rather than the block mark "M," can usually be assigned to either Tiberius II or Focas if of large module, and to Constantine III if of small module and of a clipped appearance. Finally in figure 10 we have a bronze of the 11th century showing Constantine X and his wife Eudocia standing on the obverse with Christ standing on the reverse. Although this coin can hardly be classified any better than "good," it actually is *desirable* since it is in better condition than the average such specimen.

Comments

In any work of length, it is inevitable that some errors will creep into the text despite all precautions to the contrary. This paper has been no exception. To date (June, 1954), three principle classes of errors have appeared and some explanation might be indicated. The first class of errors might be called "errors of generalization" and are inherent in any survey article. To every rule there is always an exception and Byzantine coinage is no deviant from this maxim. In the effort to reduce a vast amount of data to its commonest denominator, it was frequently necessary to make sweeping statements of fact which might not have been 100% correct. However, if note had been made of every exception to any particular rule, the paper would have been reduced to a myriad of fine details and the very purpose of the article would have been lost. The general approach would have been replaced by an academic dissertation and the grandeur of the coinage buried under a mass of petty, and often unimportant, facts.

The second error type, and the most serious, are the errors of fact. Unfortunately, a compiler is no better than his references and, in a few cases, errors of this type have been made. First, on page 12, line 16 (Jan., 1954, *Numismatist*), it was noted that the name of Antioch was changed to Theopolis by the emperor Zeno. Actually this name change took place in the early days of the reign of Justinian I and a few of his coins bear the ANT form of the mint mark rather than the later THEUP. Then, in Appendix VII-III, Part I, Tiberius III was credited with ordering the mutilation of Justinian II. Actually this took place immediately after his downfall in the reign of Leontius. Also, conflicting dates of reign were given in the text for Constantine IX and Theodora. The correct ones are in Appendix VI, Part I. Finally, on page 1296 (Dec., 1954, *Numismatist*), the sign for the 12 nummi should be XII, not XXI.

Errors of typography and oversight also are found in this paper. Some of these were intentional since it was necessary to simulate the Greek alphabet with Latin letters in the text since the proper forms were not available to the printers. Thus the letter "N" was used to indicate the Greek "pi," "O" was used for "theta" and "W" for "omega." Fortunately typographical errors have the tendency to correct themselves through repetition and need not concern us further. The errors of oversight are similar to those of typography in this respect. The majority of them resulted from failure to complete parts of stylized letters in the legends, the deficiency of a cross bar to an occasional rounded Byzantine letter "E" being the most common one. Also the failure to place the stylized "d" before several of the obverse legends of Constantine III and Constantine IV falls into this category. However, none of these is serious and all are easily found and corrected when the paper is read in its entirety. If any doubt exists, the reader can always consult the recommended texts. The important thing to keep in mind in that this is a survey paper and not a *magnum opus* of

Byzantine coinage. The legends given are only representative and not a complete listing in any case.

Acknowledgements

In conclusion, the author would like to thank the many individuals who assisted him in the preparation of the paper: the staff, especially Dr. George Miles and Henry Grunthal, of the Library and Museum of the American Numismatic Society, for providing some valuable information and for allowing the author to use Society coins as illustrations; the late Prof. A. A. Vasiliev, professor of Byzantine History at Harvard University for assisting with the historical data required for the background of the article; P. K. Anderson of Gotebo, Okla., for encouragement in preparing this paper, for the complete freedom of his library, for assistance on the Visigothic Byzantine imitative coinages, and for reading and commenting on parts of the manuscript; Louis Huber of Minneapolis, Minn., for the freedom of his library, and for reading and commenting on parts of the manuscript; Dr. Roger M. Berg of Bismarck, N. D., for allowing the author to examine the Byzantine coins in his collection; Edward Gans of Berkeley, Calif., for information, not obtainable elsewhere, on the coinages of Justinian II and Marcian; the editors of the Encyclopedia Britannica for their review of certain aspects of the Antioch-Theopolis problem; Stuart Mosher, Editor Emeritus, and Elston G. Bradfield, Editor of *The Numismatist,* for their complete cooperation and valuable suggestions during the preparation of the paper. Finally, the author would like to acknowledge the deep debt he owes the late Hugh Goodacre whose fine text, *The Handbook to the Coinage of the Byzantine Empire,* did so much to first interest him in this fascinating numismatic series. It is a source of real regret that this book has been allowed to go out of print and thus remove from circulation probably the greatest impetus to Byzantine numismatics since the turn of the century.

NOTES ON COMMON BYZANTINE BRONZE COINS

N ATTEMPT was made in an earlier paper (Lhotka, 1954) to acquaint the average collector with the possibilities of the neglected Byzantine series. The information presented, however, was general and no effort was made to differentiate coins by metals and denominations with emphasis placed on data applicable to all coins and not any one special type. It has become increasingly obvious since the paper appeared that some additional information would be desirable on Byzantine bronze coins since these issues are the least expensive of the series and consequently the ones acquired by beginners. Such a collector, even with the tables included in the East Roman paper, soon becomes lost when confronted with coins which are battered, ill struck, and whose legends seem to be completely missing or represented by only a few of the original letters. All the busts look alike, and often, other than being able to recognize the Greek numeral "M" on the reverse (in the case of a 40 nummia piece), the beginner is completely confused. If this happens too frequently, he soon feels futile and returns to a more organized and less complicated series such as Lincoln Head cents. To prevent this development this paper with additional information on Byzantine bronzes was prepared. The information presented is essentially the same as that the author uses in attributing his commoner Byzantine coins and was gleaned from various texts available on the series. A list of the principal references is included at the end of the paper if additional information is desired.

Three principal types are usually present in any bulk lot of Byzantine bronzes, the larger regular issues of the Justinianean emperors from Anastasius to Focas, the poorly struck, miserable, and often grotesque coins issued by the Heraclian emperors, and lastly the various "anonymous bronzes" of the tenth and eleventh centuries. The late Heraclian and Iconoclastic bronzes up to and including the early Macedonian issues are not common and are usually not found in bulk lots of Byzantine bronze coins. This is also true of the bronzes struck by the Paleologian emperors after the restoration of the empire in 1261.

These three common series, the Justinianean, Heraclian, and "anonymous" bronzes will be considered in order, the first two taken together as a unit. The obverse and reverse types and inscriptions will be considered including pertinent data on mint marks, officinae marks, and symbols. The practical approach is stressed and tables are used whenever possible to make the information easily available for use. The embryo Byzantine numismatist should be able to attribute 75% of his unclassified bronzes regardless of their general worn and ill struck condition with the information in this paper.

The pre-Anastasius Byzantine coinages are not considered here although such specimens are usually also found in bulk lots. The earlier East Roman paper should provide adequate data for their attribution since all legends and monograms used by the emperors from Arcadius to Zeno are listed either in the text or appendix. These coins should actually be included in the Roman series since their types and inscriptions are identical to those of Constantine and his successors. H. A. Seaby[1] in his latest Roman catalog has included these coins in that series and the information presented should aid any interested beginner. It is unfortunate that the average text on Roman coins disregards them, each claiming they belong to the other series. Consequently, a

to differentiate one emperor from another by features alone. The key to identification is primarily in the obverse legend since the reverses are again basically alike bearing only the denomination numeral, a few decorations (usually crosses or Christograms), and the mint and officina (workshop) marks. The coins of Anastasius I, Justin I, and the first issues of Justinian I are not dated. Anastasius commonly used the obverse legend DNANASTASIVSPPAVG with the bust breaking the legend between the A and the S.

Fig. 1. A 40 nummia piece of Anastasius I struck at Constantinople. The officina mark, GAMMA, indicating the third mint division is not discernible in the illustration.

numismatic blind spot has been created and the coinages from Arcadius to Zeno tend to flounder in darkness.

Obverse Types and Inscriptions on Byzantine Justinianean and Heraclian Bronze Coins

The obverse bust used by Anastasius I after his reform on the Byzantine coinage was essentially a continuation of the diademed bust right used by the Roman emperors since the fourth century. The portraits are formal and it is impossible

Fig. 2. A coin similar to Fig. 1 but struck by Justin I at the fourth officina of the same mint. By comparing the two coins, can you tell why they were attributed to these two emperors and, more important, why the second was not attributed to Justinian I?

Justin I used the legend DNIVSTINVSPPAVG (the break being between the I and the N) while Justinian's legend usually reads DNIVSTINI ANVSPPAVG. In many cases the complete legend will not be available for attribution, especially on the smaller bronzes, but often an accurate classification is possible with only a few letters available. Thus, any coin in which the letter A appears to the left of the bust can be assigned to Anastasius while one

1. Seaby, H. A. 1954. *Roman Coins and Their Values*. London.

on which an A is found immediately after the bust break will probably be of Justinian. The presence of the letter I to the left of the bust will eliminate the possibility of the coin belonging to Anastasius.

In April of 538, Justinian changed the traditional bust right to a facing bust on his bronze coins. On the new coinage the emperor was usually portrayed as helmeted (usually plumed), wearing a cuirass, and holding the globus cruciger in his right hand and in his left a shield. The legend was not changed. He

bust forms although a few coins exist on which he is shown with his wife Anastasia (Thessalonika, 20 nummia). Tiberius commonly used variations of the legend dMTIbCONS TANTPPAVI on his bronzes with two different bust styles, the imperial and the consular. The former is essentially the same as that found on the coins of Justinian while the latter, used simultaneously with the older form, depicted the emperor in consular robes and crown holding the mappa in his right hand and an eagle tipped

Fig. 3. A 20 nummia piece of the Year 10 struck at the Cyzicus mint and bearing the characteristic obverse of Justin II. No officina mark is present indicating that only one workshop was active when the coin was struck.

continued this style the remainder of his reign and in general his successors continued it on their bronze coins. Simultaneous with the bust change, Justinian introduced dating of his coins by regal year on the reverse starting with the year XII and continuing until the last year of his reign in 565.

Justin II, Justinian's nephew and successor, occasionally used bust obverses (both facing and to the right) but very early in his reign adopted a very characteristic obverse type which almost automatically assigns a coin bearing it to his reign. The bust obverses were replaced on all denominations of bronze with two seated figures in imperial robes on a double throne (Justin and his wife Sophia) with the general legend DNIVSTI NVSPPAVG. The name of Sophia was also included in the legend in a few rare cases (DN IVSTINO ETSOFIE AG — Carthage mint, 40 and 20 nummia denominations).

Tiberius Constantine, on his succession to the throne, returned to

Fig. 4. A 40 nummia piece of Tiberius showing the consular obverse. The reverse indicates that the coin was issued in the Year Seven at the Constantinople mint from the second officina.

scepter in his left hand. Often the DN was written dm. The Antioch mint struck during this reign a number of consular coins bearing completely unintelligible legends and such coins can usually be safely attributed to Tiberius if they are dated under year eight.

Maurice Tiberius, his successor, struck coins which closely resemble those of Tiberius since he used both bust types. Maurice used variations of the legends DNmAVRIC TIbER-PPAVG and DNmAVRC TIbPPAVI. At Antioch, dm often replaced DN in the legend. Superficially the issues of these emperors appear the same, especially when poorly struck or worn, but actually it is not difficult to differentiate between them. First, check the date and if it is over eight, the coin must belong to Maurice since Tiberius struck no coins dated later than 582. The location of the letters TIb offer a good clue to attribution since if they appear to the left of the bust break, the coin is probably an issue of Tiberius. Maurice did strike coins bearing the legend variant DNTIbMAV RIC-PPAVG but the chances are in favor of such coins belonging to Tiberius.

Fig. 6. A 40 nummia piece of Constantine III showing reduced size and typical crudeness of his coinage. Note the division of ANANEO on the reverse and the script denominational mark favored by this emperor.

Fig. 5. A 40 nummia piece of Heraclius struck in the Year Six at the fifth officina ("E") of the Constantinople mint. Martina, the emperor, and Heraclius Constantine form the obverse type.

Letters and letter styles will be of great help too. The presence of M or V almost automatically assigns the coin to Maurice while a stylized d rather than a standard Roman D in the *dominus nostrum* of the imperial titles tends to give the coin to Tiberius.

Maurice also struck a series of family coins at the Cherson mint depicting his wife Constantia and eldest son Theodosius. These issues are easily identified since they bear the Cherson mint mark or are of odd denominations such as the four pentanummia piece identified by a Greek letter *delta* and the eight pentanummia piece which bears the numeral *H*. They are not especially common.

Focas, Maurice's successor, used variants of the legends dMFOCAS PERPAVG and dMFOCA PERPAVG in combination with both imperial and consular busts. In addition he also struck a few standing figure coins with his wife Leonita included in the obverse type. The legends on the coins of Focas are not as important as those of his predecessors since, in contrast to the smooth shaven faces of those rulers, Focas depicts himself as bearded. Thus any coin of the style and module of the late sixth century on which a bearded bust is found is probably an issue of Focas. Also the presence of the letters F and O further aid in attributing a coin to Focas.

The Byzantine coinage underwent a steady degeneration during and following the reign of Focas and during the reign of Heraclius it became extremely crude. Legends are corrupted, unintelligible, and frequently off the flan. Thus, the importance of the legend in attributing Heraclian bronzes is greatly reduced. The obverse types of Heraclius are quite confusing since he used many family types depicting his eldest son Heraclius Constantine, his second son Heracleonas, and his second wife Martina in addition to his own likeness. The reader is referred to the attached tables of his types by denomination and by mints for more detailed information. Heraclian legends are varied when legible. dNhERACLI PERPAVG is an example of an obverse legend in the name of Heraclius alone while ddNNhERACLIVSEThERACONST-

PPAV is an example of one including the name of his eldest son.

Neither Heraclius Constantine nor Heracleonas struck coins in their own names following their father's death. However, sometimes coins of Heraclius, generally of the Carthage mint, bearing the obverse legend variants ERACLIO CONSVLI but with Greek *lambdas* substituted for the letters L are confused with issues of the eldest son.

The coins of Constantine III are even poorer than those of Heraclius if such a thing is possible. They are

legends are miserable and of little aid in attributing the coins. A popular one used by Constantine III on the obverse of his standing figure coins was EN TWTO NIKA while another found on bronzes bearing his bust was InPER CONST. In one case Constantine placed his name on the reverse of his bronze coin putting the letters KWN to the left of the 40 nummia mark and CTAN to the right. These particular coins were issued between the years 655 and 657 from the Constantinople mint.

Fig. 8. "Anonymous" coin of the Bellinger Class 3 type.

The obverse legends of the emperors following Constantine III continue to be blundered and in many cases are completely absent. Legible legends on bronze coins do not appear again until well into the Iconoclastic period. The coins of the successors of Constantine III are not common and usually do not present a problem to the average Byzantine collector. If a collector obtains a coin which does not seem to fit into the reigns mentioned, it is recommended that he consult one of the standard texts.

Fig. 7. An example of pseudo-dating on a coin of Michael II.

of small module and often clipped. He used a number of obverse types including his own bust and standing figure and more rarely those of his son and heir Constantine IV. The

OBVERSE TYPES OF THE BRONZE COINS OF HERACLIUS

TYPE A. Facing bust of Heraclius.
TYPE B. Facing busts of Heraclius (left) and Heraclius Constantine (right).
TYPE C. Facing busts of Martina (left), Heraclius (center), and Heraclius Constantine (right).
TYPE D. Facing busts of Heraclius Constantine (left), Heraclius (center), and Heracleonas (right).
TYPE E. Standing facing figure of Heraclius alone.
TYPE F. Standing facing figures of Heraclius (left) and Heraclius Constantine (right).
TYPE G. Standing facing figures of Martina (left), Heraclius (center), and Heraclius Constantine (right).
TYPE H. Standing facing figures of Heraclius Constantine (left), Heraclius (center), and Heracleonas (right).

The busts are mask-like and wear crowns surmounted with small crosses although those of Heraclius alone may be helmeted. The emperor is usually well bearded and Heraclius Constantine may also be bearded but never as heavily as his father. Martina and Heracleonas are not bearded and the former may be distinguished on some coins by her long hair. The standing figures appear similar except for size with the emperor always being depicted as taller than the others. Martina and Heraclius Constantine are usually about the same size while Heracleonas is somewhat smaller. The figures are dressed in stiff ceremonial robes and they usually hold the globus cruciger, a long cross, or other symbol of authority. Heraclius is occasionally shown wearing armor.

	CON	TES	NIKO	KYZ	ISAVR	Cyprus	THEVP	ALEZ	CART	SCLs	ROM	RAVENNA
TYPE A.	M K	K	M	M			IB	XXXX XX X V	M I V			X
TYPE B.					M	M	M IB		M I	XX		M XXXX XX K
TYPE C.												M K
TYPE D.											K	
TYPE E.							IB		K M			
TYPE F.	M Λ K	M K	M	M								M K
TYPE G.	M	M	M	M		M	IB					
TYPE H.	M											M

Reverse Types and Inscriptions on Byzantine Justinianean and Heraclian Bronze Coins

When Anastasius succeeded Zeno as ruler of the remains of the Roman empire in the East, one of his first official acts was a reform of the coinage. The solidus, the standard gold coinage unit, was divided into 6000 parts called nummia and the bronze coins were struck in multiples of the unit. The largest bronze coin issued was the 40 nummia piece and its denomination was designated by the Greek numeral M on the reverse. The smallest commonly struck bronze coin was the five nummia piece designated by the numeral E (sometimes by V) although a few smaller units were issued at Thessalonika by Justinian I. This denominational device occupied the center of the reverse and usually is boldly presented and not an entirely unattractive type. In the list of denominations by mints all of the various denominational devices are given and it is possible by consulting the tables to see exactly which denominations were issued by any particular emperor, where they were struck, and the form the denominational device took at each mint. This is especially valuable when it is clear that certain emperors preferred the script form for the 40 nummia mark (m) while others used the block form (M). The coins of Heraclius can thusly be differentiated from those of Constantine III as can those of Tiberius Constantine from Maurice Tiberius.

The mint mark, present on most of these coins of the Justinianean and Heraclian periods, is located in the exergue. The commoner mint marks used by the various active mints during these years are included in the denominational lists. The absence of such a mark in smaller denominations usually indicates the coin was struck in Constantinople. In close connection with the mint marks are the officina numerals or the marks that show in exactly which division of each mint the coin was struck. These take the forms of small Greek letters (alpha, beta, *delta*, *gamma*, *etc.)* and are located generally either below the denominational symbol (such as immediately the point of the block M on 40 nummia pieces) or incorporated into the mint mark such as CONB in which the CON shows that the coin was struck in Constantinople and the B indicates it was from the second officina or mint division. Once in a while officina marks are to the left of the field and in later years they may be absent completely.

On some of the smaller denominations characteristic mint marks are apparently absent. For example, on the 20 nummia pieces (K) of Constantinople struck by Anastasius no CON appears and the only major device present other than the denominational symbol is a long cross in the left field. This is also true of the coins of several of his suc-

cessors. At Antioch a similar problem presents itself. The mint mark THEVP is not present and the mint indicated by a small device resembling a letter P with a tail usually located in the exergue. The name of the city of Antioch was changed to Theopolis by Justinian after an earthquake in November 528 altering the mint mark from ANT (ANTIX) to THEVP.

Small symbols, mainly crosses and Christograms, are also found in the reverse fields. Anastasius commonly placed such symbols on either side of his denominational symbol and often above it. Justin I continued the practice as did Justinian until his introduction of dating. After that time the symbols to the right and left disappeared but the use of a small cross above the denominational device continued practically until the end of the Heraclian period.

TABLE OF BYZANTINE GREEK NUMERALS USED TO DESIGNATE DENOMINATIONS AND OFFICINAE SEQUENCE

1.—	**A**	5.—	**Є**	10.—	**I**	20.—	**K**
2.—	**B**	6.—	**S**	12.—	**IB**	30.—	**ᐱ**
3.—	**Γ**	7.—	**Z**	16.—	**IS**	33.—	**ᐱΓ**
4.—	**Δ**	8.—	**H**	18.—	**IH**	40.—	**M**

Approximate number of mint workshops (officinae) active at the various Byzantine mints and indicated on the bronze coins during the Justinianean and Heraclian periods (after Wroth).

Constantinople — up to five active.
Thessalonica — rarely indicated.
Nicomedia — two only.
Cyzicus — two only.
Antioch — up to five active.
Isauria — one only.
Cyprus — believed up to three.
Alexandria — none indicated.

Carthage — usually none indicated but up to five or six under Justinian I.
Sicily — no officina marks
Rome — no officina marks on bronzes.
Ravenna — rarely indicated on bronzes.
Cherson — none except on the possible coinage of Justinian I up to four.

1

2

3

4

Examples of how the 20 nummia denomination mark K was often incorporated into the mint mark. Decorative marks other than the surmounting cross are not shown. The marks indicate from left to right (1) Antioch, (2) Nicomedia, (3) Cyzicus, and (4) Antioch.

BYZANTINE BRONZE COIN DENOMINATIONS AND THEIR MINTS OF ISSUE FROM ANASTASIUS I TO TIBERIUS III.

EMPEROR	DENOMINATION IN NUMMIA	SYMBOL	Constantinople (CON)	Nicomedia (NIKO, NIK, NI, N)	Antioch (ANTIX, ANT, THEVP')	Thessalonica (THESSOB, TES, ΘES)	Cyzicus (KYZ, KY, K)	Alexandria (ALEZ)	Carthage (KART, KAR, CAR, KRTC, CT)	Sicily (also Catina & Syracuse) (SCLs, SCL, CAT, CVPAKOVCI)	Rome (ROM, RM, R)	Ravenna (RAVENNA, RAVEN, RAV, RA)	Isauria (ISAVR)	Cyprus (KνIIP')	Cherson (XEPCONOC)
Anastasius I 491-518	40	M	x	x	x										
	20	K	x	x											
	10	I	x	x											
	5	E	x		x										
Justin I 518-527	40	M	x	x	x	x	x								
	20	K	x	x	x	x	x								
	10	I	x		x										
	5	E	x		x										
Justin I with Justinian I 527	40	M	x	x	x										
	20	K			x										
	5	E			x										
Justinian I 527-565	40	M	x	x	x		x		x			x			
	33	ΛΓ								x					
	20	K	x	x	x	x	x		x						
	—	XX										x			
	16	IS				x									
	12	IB						x							
	10	I	x	x	x				x			x	x		
	—	X							x	x					
	8	H				x									
	6	S						x							
	5	E	x					x	x						
	4	Δ				x									
	3	Γ				x									
	2	B				x									
Justin II 565-578	40	M	x	x	x		x		x						
	20	K	x	x	x	x	x		x						
	—	XX										x			
	12	IB						x							
	10	I			x	x					x				
	—	X									x	x			
Tiberius II 578-582	40	M	x		x										
	—	m	x	x	x		x								
	30	XXX	x	x	x		x								
	20	K			x	x									
	—	XX	x	x	x		x					x			
	12	IB						x							
	10	I	x		x							x			
	—	X	x		x										
	5	u	x												
Maurice Tiberius 582-602	40	M	x	x	x		x					x			x
	—	XXXX								x					
	—	H													x

(H-8 pentanummia)

BYZANTINE BRONZE COIN DENOMINATIONS AND THEIR MINTS OF ISSUE FROM ANASTASIUS I TO TIBERIUS III.

EMPEROR	DENOMINATION IN NUMMIA	SYMBOL	Constantinople (CON)	Nicomedia (NIKO, NIK, NI, N)	Antioch (ANTIX, ANT, THEVP')	Thessalonica (THESSOB, TES, ΘES)	Cyzicus (KYZ, KY, K)	Alexandria (ALEZ)	Carthage (KART, KAR, CAR, KRTC, CT)	Sicily (also Catina & Syracuse) (SCLs, SCL, CAT, CVPAKOVCI)	Rome (ROM, RM, R)	Ravenna (RAVENNA, RAVEN, RAV, RA)	Isauria (ISAVR)	Cyprus (KVIIP')	Cherson (XEPCONOC)
	20	K	x		x	**X**	x		x			x			x
	—	XX							x		x	x			
	—	Δ													x
	(Δ-4 pentanummia)														
	12	IB						x							
	10	I	x		x		x		x			x			
	—	X							x	x	x				
	5	V							x	x					
	—	E	x						x						
Focas 602-610	40	m	x	x	x		x					x			
	—	XXXX	x	x		x			x			x			
	30	XXX	x	x											
	20	K				x									
	—	XX	x	x	x	x	x		x			x			
	12	IB						x							
	10	X	x		x				x			x			
	5	E							x						
	—	u	x												
Heraclius 610-641	40	M	x	x	x	x	x	x	x	x		x	x	x	
	—	XXXX							x			x			
	30	Λ	x												
	20	K	x			x			x			x	x		
	—	XX							x			x	x		
	12	IB						x							
	10	I								x					
	—	X							x			x			
	6	S						x							
	5	V							x	x					
Constantine III (Constans II) 641-668	40	M	x						x	x					
	—	m	x						x	x	x				
	—	XXXX							x						
	20	K	x							x	x				
	—	XX							x		x				
	10	I								x					
	—	X							x	x					
Constantine IV 668-685	40	M	x						x	x		x			
	—	m							x						
	20	K	x							x					
	—	XX									x				
	10	I	x												
Justinian II 685-695, 705-711	40	M	x						x	x					
	20	K	x												
Tiberius III 698-705	40	M	x							x	x				
	20	K	x												

DATING OF BYZANTINE BRONZE COINS

Justinian I

The practice of dating Byzantine bronze coins was introduced by the Emperor Justinian I in the twelfth year of his reign (538 A.D.) when he ordered that the regal year be placed to the right of the reverse denomination mark and the word ANNO (year) to the left. His dates start in 538 with the numeral XII, the same year the obverse type was changed from a bust right (on the major bronze denominations) to a facing bust.

Numeral	Regal Year	Numeral	Regal Year
12	538/9	26	552/3
13	539/40	27	553/4
14	540/1	28	554/5
15	541/2	29	555/6
16	542/3	30	556/7
17	543/4	31	557/8
18	544/5	32	558/9
19	545/6	33	559/60
20	546/7	34	560/1
21	547/8	35	561/2
22	548/9	36	562/3
23	549/50	37	563/4
24	550/1	38	564/5
25	551/2	39	565

Justin II

Justin II followed the dating custom of his uncle starting his regal years (I) with 565.

Numeral	Regal Year	Numeral	Regal Year
1	565/6	8	572/3
2	566/7	9	573/4
3	567/8	10	574/5
4	468/9	11	575/6
5	569/70	12	576/7
6	570/1	13	577/8
7	571/2		

Tiberius II

With one interesting exception, Tiberius continued the dating of his coins as had the previous emperors.

During the last years of his rule, Justin had been violently insane and the real government had been in the hands of his wife Sophia and Tiberius who had been raised to the rank of caesar by the failing Justin in 574. Thus, when Tiberius succeeded to power in 578 he preferred not to date his coins from the actual date of his reign but rather from his "caesarship" in 574 making the year 578/9 the year five. However, an odd series of consular coins exist from the Antioch mint dated from the year one and are complete to year eight. Two reasons are offered for this variation, one being that the mint officials at Antioch, on hearing that Tiberius had become emperor and knowing he planned to date from year five, struck this series to give him a full date list, the other theory being that these dates involve a complex method of determining years of consulship (see Wroth).

Numeral	Regal Year	Numeral	Regal Year
5	578/9	7	580/1
6	579/80	8	581/2

Maurice Tiberius

Maurice again continued the regal year method of dating his coins counting the year of his elevation to power, 582, as year one. This technique is followed at all mints with the exception of a few coins dated by indictions[2] struck at Carthage (see Wroth).

Numeral	Regal Year	Numeral	Regal Year
1	582/3	12	593/4
2	583/4	13	594/5
3	584/5	14	595/6
4	585/6	15	596/7
5	586/7	16	597/8
6	587/8	17	598/9
7	588/9	18	599/600
8	589/90	19	600/1
9	590/1	20	601/2
10	591/2	21	602
11	592/3		

---

2. The dating of coins by indictions is discussed in detail by Philip Grierson in the 1950 *Numismatic Chronicle* (Sixth Series, Nos. 37-38) in his paper "Dated Solidi of Maurice, Phocas, and Heraclius." In the same issue, he considers at length the "Consular" coinages struck at the African mints in the name of Heraclius offering the interesting suggestion that the two figures depicted (on those coins typified by

Focas

The regal year dating of coins continued as previously and although Focas made other changes in style and denomination markings, his coins are dated by regal years one to eight.

Numeral	Regal Year	Numeral	Regal Year
1	602/3	5	606/7
2	603/4	6	607/8
3	604/5	7	608/9
4	605/6	8	609/10

Heraclius

Heraclius dated his coins much the same as the previous emperors. On those coins dated years one to three, we find the emperor usually depicted alone. Then in year three and to year five, Heraclius Constantine is also shown. His second wife, Martina, is placed on the bronze coins from year six to 19. In year 20 and for years onward Heraclius is shown in military dress with Heraclius Constantine while in year 30 (earlier on some provincial coins) Heracleonas joins his father and brother as an obverse type on the bronze issued at the main mint in Constantinople.

Numeral	Regal Year	Numeral	Regal Year
1	610/1	17	626/7
2	611/2	18	627/8
3	612/3	19	628/9
4	613/4	20	629/30
5	614/5	21	630/1
6	615/6	22	631/2
7	616/7	23	632/3
8	617/8	24	633/4
9	618/9	25	634/5
10	619/20	26	635/6
11	620/1	27	262/7
12	621/2	28	637/8
13	622/3	29	638/9
14	623/4	30	639/40
15	624/5	31	640/1
16	625/6		

Constantine III

Constantine followed the general scheme of dating established by the earlier emperors but the coinage degenerated rather badly during his reign. The dating is often only spasmodic and is missing in a great many cases. Some years are missing from all of the mints.

Numeral	Regal Year	Numeral	Regal Year
1	641/2	15	655/6
2	642/3	16	656/7
3	643/4	17	657/8
4	644/5	18	658/9
5	645/6	19	659/60
6	646/7	20	660/1
7	647/8	21	661/2
8	648/9	22	662/3
9	649/50	23	663/4
10	650/1	24	664/5
11	651/2	25	665/6
12	652/3	26	666/7
13	653/4	27	667/8
14	654/5		

The dating of coins essentially stops after the reign of Constantine III. A few coins of Constantine IV are dated, usually year 30, with the regal year calculated from 654, the year he was associated in the government by his father Constantine III. Although a few dated coins appear early in the Iconoclastic period (such as the 30 year pieces of Constantine V) the bulk of the dating on these bronzes is pseudo-dating. Irene, Nicephorus I, Michael I, Leo V, and Michael II all struck coins bearing the numerals XXX to one side of the denominational mark and NNN on the other side. Experts now believe this to be a cryptic reference to the Trinity since none of these ruled over 10 years. Theophilus, on succeeding his father Michael II, also struck this type of bronze in the 40 nummia denomination, but later in his reign introduced a new reverse type utilizing a four line inscription (✚ ΘEO / FILEAVG / OCSTESV/ NICAS) eliminating the traditional denominational marks of Anastasius I. By the reign of John I when the so-called anonymous series was introduced. The emperor's name was omitted from these

---

two facing obverse busts) are not the Emperor Heraclius and his eldest son, Heraclius Constantine, but rather the Emperor-to-be Heraclius (to the left) and his father, the Exarch of Africa Heraclius (to the right).

"anonymous" coins and the obverse and reverse were occupied by portraits of the Holy Family and inscriptions proclaiming the "King of Kings."

NUMERAL FORMS

The numerals used to indicate the regal years by which the great bulk of the early Byzantine bronze coins are dated are essentially Roman in style in contrast to the Greek letters used to determine denominations. As previously noted the date is placed to the right of the denomination symbol while the word ANNO is to the left. On the coins of Constantine III this arrangement was sometimes modified and the word ANANEO was split with ANA to the left and NEO to the right. Under these conditions the date is not necessarily present. Too, sometimes the ANA-NEO was placed across the top of the coin with the date in its usual place. A representative list of numeral forms is shown here so that the various arrangements of the individual numerals can be shown. As can be seen, contrary to what might be suspected, the old Roman numeral V appears but seldom and then mainly in the earlier years of the Byzantine era. The numeral IV for four is never used but rather is expressed as IIII. The exact sequence of numerals in the higher numbers is quite irregular. Thus the numeral for 13 may be expressed IIIX or XIII. Two new numerals for five and six appear both looking like a small case letter u but with the one representing six being more closed at the top. Thus the number seven may be expressed in terms of "five plus 2" at one mint and "six plus one" at another mint. Vertical arrangements are extremely common, especially in the higher series of regal years such as in Justinian's later years. Again the sequence may be irregular. Coins dated by indictions are most likely to be encoun-

REPRESENTATIVE NUMERAL FORMS USED TO INDICATE REGAL YEARS DURING THE JUSTINIAN AND HERACLIAN PERIODS

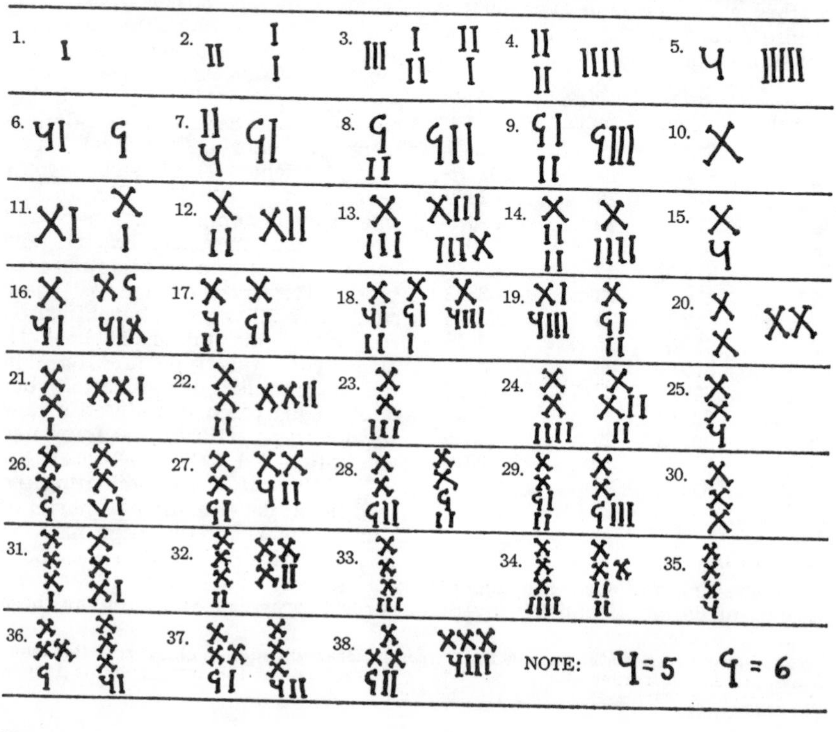

NOTE: Ч = 5   Ϛ = 6

tered by the beginner in the series issued by Maurice at Carthage although Constantine III did strike coins dated in this manner. Examples of Carthage issues of Maurice so dated are a 20 nummia piece with the legend INDIII (Indictio III) in the reverse exergue (584/5) and a 10 nummia piece with INDS (Indictio VI) in the obverse exergue (587/8). 10 (I) and five (V) nummia pieces also show this form of dating. Constantine III issued an unusual series in which Greek letters appear to be included in the date. The reader is referred to Wroth for his explanation of this arrangement since it is somewhat beyond our general scope.

Overstriking was again popular during the Macedonian and Comnenian "anonymous" era and many of these coins will show traces of previous inscriptions. The study of overstrikes is extremely important in this series since it has been one of the principal methods of determining the proper sequence in which these coins were issued.

It is of value to remember when examining overstruck Byzantine coins that the dies were usually (but not always) aligned ↑↓ so that the obverse and reverse faces possessed

Fig. 9. A large bronze of Constantine X, probably the commonest of the "named" bronzes found with "anonymous" Byzantine coins of the tenth and eleventh centuries.

OVERSTRIKES AND COUNTERMARKS

Overstruck coins are fairly common in the Byzantine series, principally during the Heraclian era and then again later during the period when the "anonymous" coins were issued. The Heraclian overstrikes are usually found on 40 nummia pieces where Heraclius placed his own types and inscriptions over those of a previous ruler, generally Focas or Maurice Tiberius or Constantine III overstruck the coins of Heraclius. Frequently much of the former design is still visible and it is possible to determine exactly the name of the previous emperor, the mint where the coin was struck, and even the date of issue. Sometimes a coin might be overstruck several times and portions of three or even four former types and inscriptions are present on the coin's surfaces.

Fig. 10. One of the real pleasures of collecting an obscure series is the occasional opportunity of acquiring rarities at nominal prices. Here is one such coin, a 30 nummia bronze of Focas struck in the years 607/608 at the first officina of the Nicomedia mint. The author found this in a large batch of unclassified sixth century coins.

the same inverse orientation found on U.S. coins. Consequently, if there are traces of several strikings on a coin, the proper obverses and reverses may be very simply paired. Orient one of the types (it doesn't matter which face is used) so that it is upright. Then turn the coin over and the other face will also be upright. This is an especially valuable maneuver when one face is quite distinct but only traces remain of the other type. The Heraclian overstrikes, due to the decreased die size, usually show traces of the outer portions of the coin on which they were struck. On the obverse, parts of the old dotted border, portions of the legend (usually the first few letters), the plume of the emperor's helmet or the cross of his crown may remain, while on the reverse the word ANNO, the date, and the mint mark (which may differ from the new one) may still be visible. On weakly overstruck coins, the former denominational mark may still be visible beneath the new symbol, especially on the overstruck XXXX coins of Focas. The "anonymous" series overstrikes are more difficult to decipher since the size differentiation does not exist and it is sometimes difficult to decide which is the superimposed type. When there is only one overstrike this is not too hard to do but it can become tricky when there are three or more overstrikes present. Since obverses were not necessarily restruck on obverses the new obverse may be found superimposed on an old reverse. This too can cause confusion.

Countermarks are not especially common in the Byzantine bronze series but two fairly common examples do exist, the overstrikes of Heraclius for Sicily and a series of coins, principally from Constantinople, overstruck by Constantine III. The former coins, all countermarked with a Sicily mint mark SCLs, etc. or with a monogram of Heraclius, or even his bust (or busts of the emperor and eldest son), are usually of earlier rulers but some examples of his own coins so countermarked do exist. The latter group consists of a number of coins generally bearing the Constantinople mint mark and countermarked with the monogram of Constantine III, an anchor like device with the letter K on the shaft.

ANONYMOUS BRONZE BYZANTINE SERIES

Bronze coins of the rulers succeeding Constantine III are not particularly common until the introduction of the "anonymous" series by John I in the mid-tenth century, so called because the emperors replaced their names on these coins with the name of Christ. Needless to say, trying to place this group accurately in proper sequence has been a popular pastime of Byzantine numismatists for years. Although the nineteenth century Byzantine scholars such as Sabatier and Tolstoi made some suggestions, the first serious attempt to attribute the various types in the series to specific emperors was made by Wroth in his British Museum catalog published in 1908. His attributions were accepted for many years and many still prefer them. However, in 1928 Bellinger published his A.N.S. monograph in which he reviewed the Wroth classifications and suggested a revised list of attributions which are used by American numismatists today. It is most interesting to note that the Bellinger lists are now under attack by Whitting and Piper who have issued a still different sequence of strikings but have not yet suggested specific imperial attributions. The classifications of Bellinger, Wroth, and Whitting and Piper are all listed in the tables and the reader may take his choice. These, of course, are not the only attributions of the "anonymous" series but were selected as the most representative. If interested, the reader can find excellent papers on this subject in almost all of the learned numismatic journals. For example, Margaret Thompson (*The Athenian Agora, II, Coins: Roman-Venetian*, Princeton, 1954) suggests the following attributions of the "anonymous" series based on the study of overstrikes in a large hoard of such coins found in the Agora excavations at Athens:

Class A (Bellinger Class 1) — John I (small module), Basil II & Constantine VIII (large module); Class B (B — 2) — Romanus III; Class C (B — 3) — Michael IV; Class D (B — 6) — Constantine XI; Class E (B — 4) — Isaac I; Class F (B — 5) — Constantine X; Class G (B — 7) — Romanus IV; Class H (B — 8) — Michael VII; Class I (B — 9) — Nicophorus III; Classes J, K, and L (B — 10, 11, and 13) — Alexius I.

Miss Thompson's attributions are supported by Whitting in the 1955 *Numismatic Chronicle* ("The Anonymous Byzantine Bronze," pp. 89-98) and may prove a strong contender to replace the older, but more popular, attributions of Wroth and Bellinger.

The numismatic detective work involved in the "anonymous" studies is extremely fascinating and the reader might find it worth his while to read the original articles and see how these men have approached the matter. It is problems of this type that have done much to make Byzantine numismatics one of the more interesting series available for study.

BYZANTINE ANONYMOUS BRONZE COINAGES
CLASSIFICATIONS AND ATTRIBUTIONS

Types and Inscriptions	Bellinger	Wroth (BMC)	Whitting & Piper
Obverse: Bearded, facing bust of Christ wearing nimbus cruciger, tunic, mantle, and holding book of Gospels in left hand, right raised in benediction. Legend—EMMANOVHΛ. In field IC XC.	Class I Small module: John I. (969-973)	Class I Pellets (one or two) in limbs of cross of nimbus: John I.	Class a
Reverse: Inscription in four lines. +IhSUS XRISTuS bASILEu bASILE	Large module: Basil II and Constantine VIII. (976-1025) Large module with squares in limbs of nimbus crosses: Romanus III. (1028-1034)	Crosses in limbs of nimbus cross: Basil II and Constantine VIII. Crescents in limbs of nimbus crosses: Constantine VIII alone. (1025-1028) Squares in limbs of nimbus crosses: Romanus III.	
Obverse: Similar to above but with two pellets and square in limbs of nimbus crosses.	Class 2 Michael IV (1034-1041)	Class II Michael IV	Class b
Reverse: Inscription in three lines but arranged in the angles of a Latin cross standing on three steps. IS XS bAS ILE bAS ILE			
Obverse: Inscription as above but half figure of Christ replaces the bust. One pellet is in each limb of cross in nimbus.	Class 3 Constantine IX (1042-1055)	Class III Theodora (1055-1056)	Class c
Reverse: Arranged in the			

limbs of a jewelled cross:

$$\overline{IC}\ \overline{XC}$$

$$\overline{NI}\ \overline{KA}$$

| Obverse: Similar to Bellinger Class 1 but both hands hold book and there are two pellets in each limb of nimbus cross.

Reverse: Inscription in three lines. Above inscription cross, below crescent.

    IX XS
    bASILE
    bASIL | Class 4
Theodora | Class VI

Isaac I
(1057-1059) | Class f |

| Obverse: Christ, bearded, seated facing on a *backless* throne wearing tunic, mantle, right hand raised in benediction, left holding book of Gospels. Nimbus cruciger is plain.

Reverse: Inscription in three lines. Cross above and below the inscription.

    ISXS
    bASILE
    bASIL | Class 5

Michael VI
(1056-1057) | Class IV

Michael VI | Class g |

| Obverse: As above but seated on a throne *with a back* and with a pellet in each limb of the nimbus cross.

Reverse: Inscription in three lines. A cross above and a crescent below the inscription.

    ISXS
    bASILE
    bASIL | Class 6

Isaac I | Class V

Constantine X
(1059-1067) | Class d |

| Obverse: Bust of Christ as in Bellinger Class 1 but plain nimbus, no legend other than $\overline{ICXC}$. Border of large dots.

Reverse: Bust of the Virgin, *orans,* wearing nimbus, veil, mantle, $\overline{MP\theta V}$ in field. Border of large dots. | Class 7

Michael VII
(1071-1078) | Class VII

Constantine IX | Class h |

Obverse: Bust of Christ, bearded, facing, one pellet in limbs of nimbus cross otherwise as in Bellinger Class 1. No legend, except $\overline{IC}$ $\overline{XC}$.	Class 11	Class VIII	Class i
	Alexius I (1081-1118)	Constantine IX or Michael VII	
Reverse: Half length figure of Virgin, facing orans, wearing nimbus, mantle, veil. $\overline{MP}$ $\overline{\Theta V}$ of M O in field.			

The following classes of Bellinger were attributed by Wroth to the Latin emperors and he did not consider them as true Byzantine coins.

Obverse: Bust of Christ as in Class 1 but with X in limbs of nimbus cross. $\overline{IC}$ $\overline{XC}$ in field.	Bellinger Class 8
Reverse: Patriarchal cross with one large and two small pellets at each upper extremity; at base large pellet with floral ornaments to left and right.	Struck by Alexius for the crusaders.
Obverse: Similar to Class 8 but with only one pellet in each limb of the nimbus cross.	Bellinger Class 9
Reverse: Latin cross with one large and two small pellets at each upper extremity; at base floral ornaments and large pellet as in Class 8. An X in the center of the cross.	Struck by Alexius for the crusaders.
Obverse: As in Class 8 but with large cross behind Christ's head with five pellets in each limb and a crescent between each limb.	Bellinger Class 10
Reverse: Latin cross as in Class 9 but with large crescent at base of cross curving upward.	Struck by Alexius for the crusaders.
Obverse: As in Class 11.	Bellinger Class 12
Reverse: Cross of four equal limbs with pellet at each extremity. Floral ornaments at base and above to left and right crescents. In center of cross an X.	Struck by Alexius for the crusaders.
Obverse: As in Class 12.	Bellinger Class 13
Reverse: Small cross pattee. Above IC, below XC; to left NI, to right KA.	Struck by Alexius for the crusaders.

In any lot of "anonymous" Byzantine coins several varieties of large module "named" bronzes struck during the same period will usually be found and the following table will assist to identify them:

Emperor	Obverse	Reverse
Constantine X (1059-1067)	Standing figures of the emperor and empress holding between them a labarum.	Standing figure of Christ.
	Bust of Constantine facing.	Bust of Christ facing.
Romanus IV (1067-1071)	Bust of Christ facing.	The imperial initials: C, R, P, *delta* arranged in the angles of a cross.
	Bust of Romanus facing.	Bust of Eudocia facing.

Michael VII (1071-1078)	Bust of Michael facing.	Bust of Christ facing.
Nicephorus III (1078-1081)	Bust of Christ facing.	The imperial initials: C, *phi*, N, and *delta* arranged in the angles of a cross with a star of eight rays in the center.

These coins usually have legends in connection with the imperial busts but they are generally almost obliterated. Sometimes it is possible to detect a few of the initial letters in the obverse legends and thus Constantine (KWN, etc.) can be differentiated from Michael (MIXAH, etc.) and Romanus (PWMAN, etc.).

Sometimes the smaller module issues of the later Comnenian rulers mainly those of Alexius I (1081-1118), John II (1118-1143), and even Manuel I (1143-1180) are found mixed with these larger "named" coins. These generally have an imperial bust or half figure on the obverse and a variety of reverses ranging from imperial initials to busts of Christ. If the first few letters of the obverse legend can be detected, attribution to emperor is easy. A indicates Alexius, IW, John and MAN assigns the coin to Manuel. If the obverse legend is not visible, it is necessary to attribute them on the basis of the reverse types and inscriptions and the reader should consult one of the more detailed texts. Occasionally a scyphate bronze, usually of Alexius III, will be found in bulk lots. Again the reader should consult the detailed texts.

IMITATIONS OF BYZANTINE COINS

Occasionally in bulk lots of Justinianean bronzes, coins will be found that just do not seem "right" for the Byzantine series. Customarily these coins are of small module (roughly one centimeter or less in diameter) and have the emperor's bust (Anastasius I, Justin I, Justinian I or even fifth century rulers) as the obverse type. The legend is incomplete or absent. The reverse is occupied with imperial monograms, nummis marks (usually V, E, or X — sometimes wreathed), or symbols such as stars, Christograms, etc. On first sight, they appear to be issues of the Constantinople mint but closer examination gives one the impression that something is "wrong" with the coins. The fabric seems improper and the workmanship unnecessarily crude. The lettering in the legends is especially bad. What the collector has acquired is usually a so-called barbaric imitation of the true Byzantine series, a coin struck by the Vandals in Africa or, more commonly, by the Ostrogoth kings in Italy. Since both of these tribes technically acknowledged the East Roman emperor as the supreme ruler, his bust was placed on the obverse of their coins even though the emperor had no real power over the kingdoms. In fact, the barbarian nations and the imperial forces were often actually at war with each other. These coinages ended when Justinian I regained Italy and Africa for the empire in the sixth century. Other barbaric imitations exist but they are so rare that no mention of them is necessary. The Arabs also copied the Byzantine bronze coinages when they swarmed over the Near East but these are easily distinguished from the real thing since they have Arabic inscriptions. This is also true of the Seljuk Turk imitations of the tenth and eleventh centuries. For additional information on these imitative series, see Parts III and IV of the "Introduction to East Roman Coinage" *(Numismatist, 1954, 1955).*

CONCLUSION

The real key to the identification of Byzantine bronze coins lies in the coins themselves since careful examination of each specimen is vital to proper attribution. These coins, because of their condition can not usually be classified completely at a single glance although it is generally not difficult to attribute them to the proper emperors. Each coin should be studied in detail both with the eye alone and with a low power glass before attempting a final classification. It may be necessary to use oblique lighting or to polish the face with a bit of inert wax to highlight a poorly defined detail. The collector must have some knowledge of Byzantine types and inscriptions since disorganized examinations are worthless and may even be misleading. These coins are not "proof" specimens. If anything they are the exact opposite but this very point is one of the fascinations of the series. Anyone with only the slightest knowledge of numismatics can accurately identify almost any U.S. coin or English issue of recent years, but it takes time, patience, and a willingness to go slowly and learn fundamentals to acquire the knowledge necessary to approach the Byzantine bronzes. What is even more rewarding, is that with time the collector will actually be able to classify accurately these coins, regardless of their miserable condition, without referring to textbooks, something that is almost impossible with other medieval and ancient series, such as the feudal French deniers or Greek imperial bronzes. Byzantine bronzes offer a real challenge to the collector who is becoming discouraged with the monotony of many of the modern coin series. If such a person is willing to accept the requisites of approaching the field, he will find in this series at a comparatively low price a source of pleasure that is found in few other coinages.

ACKNOWLEDGEMENTS

The author would like to thank the American Numismatic Society for allowing him to use certain of their coins to illustrate this paper, Drs. John Walker and J.P.C. Kent of the British Museum for information on certain coinages of the Byzantine Empire, P. K. Anderson of Oklahoma City for reading and commenting on the manuscript, and Elston G. Bradfield, Editor of *The Numismatist,* for his co-operation in preparing this paper for publication.

PRINCIPAL REFERENCES

ACKERMAN, J. 1834. *A Descriptive Catalogue of Rare and Unedited Roman Coins.* Vol. 2. Wilson, London.

BELLINGER, A. 1928. *The Anonymous Byzantine Bronze Coinage.* Monograph No. 35, American Numismatic Society.

GOODACRE, H. 1931. *Handbook to the Coinage of the Byzantine Empire.* Part II. Anastasius to Michael VI. Spink and Son, London.

KENT, P. 1954. Personal communication.

LHOTKA, J. 1954. "Introduction to East Roman Coinage. Part I, Byzantium." *Numismatist, 67,* 4-20, 137-47, 453-64.

SABATIER, J. 1862. *Description General des Monnaies Byzantines.* Two volumes. Paris.

WHITTING, P. and PIPER, C. 1952. "Overstrikes in the Byzantine Anonymous Bronze Series." *Coin and Medal Bulletin,* 377-81.

WROTH, W. 1908. *Catalogue of the Imperial Byzantine Coins in the British Museum.* Two volumes. London.

DEFINITIONS OF DENOMINATIONS

Not much attention was paid to Byzantine metrology and debasements in the East Roman text since the author felt this properly belonged in more advanced references. However, in recent years, works on the Byzantine series have tended to use terms not explained in this book, especially in naming of certain denominations, with changes resulting from coinage reforms. This additional material, based mainly on information from Sear and Whitting, should help correct these omissions. To simplify matters, the data will be presented in the form of denomination definitions.

NUMMUS (pl. NUMMIA or NUMMI, depending on the author) — The basic unit of coinage in bronze or copper of the reforms of Anastasius. By the reign of Justinian I there were 7200 such units in the solidus. Coins were usually struck in multiples of 5 (denomination mark: E or V) but even a 1 nummia coin has been described. Provincial mints were the ones that tended to strike odd values such as the 12 nummia pieces at Alexandria and the 8 nummia coins of Cherson.

FOLLIS (pl. FOLLES or FOLLEIS, again depending on author) — the standard bronze coin usually valued at 40 nummia (denomination mark: M or XXXX). One should not confuse this coin with the old Roman follis of the coinage reforms of Diocletian. The value mark of "M" disappeared during the Iconoclastic period.

SILIQUA — intially a Roman coin with its origins in the 4th century it was carried over into the Byzantine coinage valued at 24 to the solidus (period of Justinian). It was rarely issued from the eastern mints but is found struck by western mints in full, half and quarter values as well as bearing nummia values on the reverse: 250 (CN), 125 (PKE) and 120 (PK). It was also issued at double value and then called the MILLIARENSE.

HEXAGRAM — a silver coin introduced by Heraclius valued at 1/12 of a solidus. The last emperor to strike it to any degree was Constantine IV. It was a rather large coin and usually had a cross potent type on the reverse.

MILLIARESION — a silver coin with a chracteristic large flan and with a legend usually in 4 or 5 lines bearing the Imperial names with a cross potent, usually on 3 steps, as the reverse type. It was introduced by Leo III to replace the hexagram and was struck into the 11th century.

SOLIDUS (pl. SOLIDI) — the standard gold coin struck for centuries at the weight of 72 to the pound of gold. It was replaced during the reign of Nicephorus II and totally disappeared after the reforms of Alexius I. The original weight was maintained until about the reign of Basil II. In the early period from about the reign to Justinian I to Justinian II, a series of light weight solidi were issued having a value of 20 to 23 siliquae (the normal value being 24 siliquae). Why they were struck is still not really known, but since they are usually found beyond the Byzantine frontiers, it has been suggested that they acted as "trade coins".

SEMISSIS AND TREMISSIS (pl. SEMISSES, TREMISSES) — the 1/2 and 1/3 values of the solidus. The tremissis was the common gold coin struck by the barbarians during the Dark Ages and before the reforms of the Frankish king, Pepin. The last issues of these fractional coins was by Basil I and his sons, Leo VI and Alexander.

HYPERPERON or HYPERPYRON (pl. HYPERPERA OR HYPERPYRA) — the gold coin issued after the reforms of Alexius I. In addition to the hyperperon itself, two fractional units existed—the electrum ASPRON TRACHY and the billon ASPORON TRACHY valued respectively at 1/3 and 1/48 of the hyperperon. The term "aspron trachy" means "white scyphate" (cup shaped) with the word "coin" being understood. In the original East Roman text all scyphate coins were simply indicated by metal and "trachy" was not used. Following its establishment by Alexius I, the hyperperon underwent debasement at regular intervals. During the Crusader period, Nicaea issued true silver trachea (plural for trachy). Andronicus II debased the hyperperon and the last issues were under John V and John VI. In the dying years of Byzantium, the coinage was in theory based on a silver hyperperon, this last being a flat coin resembling western issues. It is also found in fractional forms along with some bronze issues.

MINT CITIES AND MINT MARKS

Another aspect of Byzantine coinage that has changed since the days of Wroth is the location of the mint cities and their mint marks. In **East Roman Coinage**, 18 mints are listed, two of which are actually western mints that struck coins in the name of the eastern emperor. Sear lists 27 mints, all striking coins (not at the same time of course) after the reforms of Anastasius. In addition to the mints listed in this text, mints are believed to have existed in Alexandretta (near Antioch), Carthagena (Spain), Corinth (Greece), Magnesia (Asia Minor during the Nicaean period), Naples and Perugia (both in Italy), Nicosia (13th century Cyprus), Philippopolis (Thrace), Salona (Dalmatia), and Sardinia (believed extension of the Carthage mint after the city's fall to the Arabs). Most of these mints were in operation for intervals prior to the Iconoclastic era, especially during the expansions of Justinian I. Specific mint marks do not exist for these cities and attribution must be made by other means such as fabric, letter forms, etc. There is a better understanding of officina marks today as well but all of this information is better found in advanced references. The beginner should merely be aware that such things exist. Wroth in his catalogues handled the matter of coins which did not fit into the accepted pattern by ascribing them to "a provincial mint". It was diplomatic and safe approach.

During the chaos of the 4th Crusade during which the crusaders seized Constantinople, a large number of base scyphate coins appeared. Their final attribution was the result of a brilliant piece of numismatic research by Michael Hendy (Dumbarton Oaks publication 12). By carefully comparing these pieces and making evaluations, Hendy came to interesting conclusions. In summary, he found that true Imperial pieces were struck from billon (chemical assay was necessary to find the silver in the coins since they all appear to be struck in copper), these coins were of a better fabric and style, the die engraving was superior, and they were well struck. Even if of small diameter they had legends that were not blundered. Most of the better coins were attributed to Alexius III struck between 1195 and 1203 and can be considered debased forms of the billon trachy, now valued at 1/184th of the hyperperon. The Bulgars are credited with striking imitatives using types typical of Manuel I, Issac II and Alexius III. The crusaders occupying Constantinople issued 20 types of these base trachea while the Greek rulers of initially Epirus and then Thessalonika struck 10 types. A few base tetartera, 3 types, also exist, one issued by the ruler at Constantinople and two from Thessalonika. The Nicaean rulers are not believed involved in these issues and when they eventually under Michael VIII recaptured Constantinople, the coinage returned to proper form. Two types of the base trachea exist, a large size one and a smaller form. Initially many felt the smaller coin was a fractional of the larger one but Hendy's work indicates that they are not. The two sizes existed apparently with equal value. One should consult Hendy's work for exact details of this interesting imitative coinage.

BIBLIOGRAPHY AND SELECTED READING

ACKERMAN, J. 1834. A descriptive Catalogue of Rare and Unedited Coins, 2 vols. London.

ADELSON, H.L. 1957. Light Weight Solidi and Byzantine Trade during the Sixth and Seventh Centuries. American Numismatic Society NNM no. 138, New York.

ADELSON, H.L. 1958. Silver Currency and Values in the Early Byzantine Empire. Centennial Publication of the American Numismatic Society, New York. pp. 1-22.

ADELSON, H.L. and G.L. KUSTAS. 1960. A Bronze Hoard of the Period of Leo I. Museum Notes of the American Numismatic Society, no. 9, pp. 139-188. New York.

AVI-JONAH, M. 1958. The Economics of Byzantine Palestine. Israel Exploration Journal, vol. 8, pp. 139-188.

BATES, G.E. 1971. Byzantine Coins. Archeological Exploration of Sardis.

BAYNES, N. 1943. The Byzantine Empire (University Home Library). Oxford Press, London.

BAYNES, N. and MOSS, H. 1949. Byzantium. Oxford Press. London

BELLINGER, A. 1928. The Anonymous Byzantine Bronze Coinage. ANS Monograph no. 35 American Numismatic Society, New York.

BELLINGER, A. and P. GRIERSON. 1966-73. Catalogue of Byzantine coins in the Dumbarton Oaks Collection and in the Whittemore Collection. vol. I (1968); vol. II in 2 parts (1968); vol. III in 2 parts (1973). Harvard Press. THIS SERIES IS NOW THE DEFINITIVE REFERENCE FOR THE BYZANTINE COINAGE.

BERG, J. 1963. Constantinople - City of God and Gold. Numismatic Scrapbook, vol. 29, pp. 1886-1890.

BERK, HARLAN 1987, Roman Gold Coins of the Medieval World 383-1453 AD.

BRADLEY, H. 1899. The Goths. G.P. Putnam, London.

BRECKENRIDGE, J.D. 1959. The Numismatic Iconography of Justinian II, 685-695 and 705-711 A.D. American Numismatic Society.

CERVIN, D. 1987. Collecting Regally-dated Byzantine Coins. World Coins. May issue. (supplement to Coin World).

FINLAY, G. 1877. A History of Greece, 7 vols. Clarendon Press, Oxford.

GALAVARIS, C.P. 1958. The Symbolism of the Imperial Costume as Displayed on Byzantine Coins. American Numismatic Society Museum Notes 8, pp. 99-117. New York.

GIBBON, E. 1946. The Decline and Fall of the Roman Empire. Edited by J.B. Bury, 3 vols. Heritage Press, New York. This work was first published in the 18th century and this is one of the more recent excellent republications. It should be required reading for anyone interested in the Byzantine World.

GOODACRE, H. 1957. A Handbook of the Coinage of the Byzantine Empire, Spink and Sons, London. This is the annotated edition reprinted by Spink in response to collectors wishes—and incidentally, it is the book that first influenced the author in this series.

GRIERSON, P. 1950. Dated Solidi of Maurice, Phocas and Heraclius. Numismatic Chronicle (6th series) vol. 10, pp. 49-70, pls. 3-4. London.

GRIERSON, P. 1961. Coinage and Money in the Byzantine Empire 498-1090. Settimane di Studio del Centro di Studi Sull' Alto Medio Eve VIII (Moneta c scambi nell'Alto Medioeve) pp. 411-453.

GRIERSON, P. 1961. Notes on the Fineness of the Byzantine Solidus. Byzantinische Zeitschrift. vol. 53, pp. 91-97.

GRIERSON, P. 1982. BYZANTINE COINS. Methuen, London.

HEISS, A. 1872. Description Generale des Monnaies de Rois Wisigotha d'Espagne. l'Imprimerie Nationale, Paris.

HENDY, M. 1969. Coinage and Money in the Byzantine Empire 1081-1261. Dumbarton Oaks Studies no. 12, Harvard University Press.

HIGGIE, W. 1964. The Byzantine Empire: Its Coinage is a Study of Christian Portraiture and Symbolism. Numismatic News, vol. 12, no. 11, p. 5, May 25 issue.

HILL, G. 1899. Handbook of Greek and Roman Coins. MacMillan, New York.

JOHNSON, A. and L. WEST. 1949. Byzantine Egypt: Economic Studies. Princeton University Press p. 344 (reprint edition 1968).

LANE-POOLE, S. 1892, Coins and Medals. Elliot Stock, London.

LARSEN, M. 1955. The Metrolog of the Coinage of Trebizond. Seaby's Coin and Medal Bulletin, no. 466 (July) pp. 270-271.

LONGUET, H. 1961. Introduction a la Numismatique Byzantine. Spink and Son, Ltd. London.

MALTHER, J. 1968. Byzantine Numismatic Bibliography. Argonaut. Chicago.

MATEO Y LLOPES, F. 1936. Catalogo de las Monedas Previsigodas y Visigodas Cabinete Numismatico de Museo Arqueologico Nacional. Madrid.

MATTINGLY, H. 1927. A Guide to the Exhibition of Roman Coins in the British Musuem. Oxford Press, London.

METCALF, D. 1965. Coinage in the Balkans 820-1355 (reprinted by Argonaut, Chicago 1966)

MILES, G. 1952. The Coinage of the Visigoths of Spain. Leovigild to Achaia II. American Numismatic Society, New York.

OMAN, C. 1898. The Byzantine Empire. G.P. Putnam, London.

OSTROGORSKY, G. 1956. History of the Byzantine State. Blackwell, Oxford.

RYNEARSON, S. 1967. Byzantine Coin Values. Malther-Westerfield, San Clemente, California.

SABATIER, J. 1862. Description General des Monnaies Byzantine. 2 vols. Paris.

SEAR, D. 1988. Byzantine Coins and Their Values. B.A. Seaby, Ltd. London. (As an intermediate text this book is probably one of the best. The values quoted for coins still bear some relationship to their present prices (1988) which cannot be said for other references).

SERGEANT, L. 1898. The Franks. T. Fisher Unwin. London.

STEARNS, J. and V. HALL. 1963. Byzantine Gold Coins from the Dartmouth College Collection. Dartmouth College Library. Hanover, New Hampshire.

THOMSEN, C. 1873-1876. Description des Monnaies du moyen Age. Copenhagen.

VASILIEV, A.A. 1952. History of the Byzantine Empire. University of Wisconsin Press, Madison.

WHITTING, P. and PIPER, C. 1952. Overstirkes in the Byzantine Anonymous Bronze Series. Seaby's Coin and Medal Bulletin, 377-381. London.

WHITTING, P. 1973. Byzantine Coins. Barnes and Jenkins, London (World of Numismatics Series).

WROTH, W. 1908 Catalogue of Imperial Byzantine Coins in the British Museum. 2 vols. London.

WROTH, W. 1911. Coins and the Vandals, Ostrogoths and Lombards and the Empires of Thessalonica, Nicaea and Trebizond in the British Museum. London.

SPECIAL ILLUSTRATIONS

1. Solidus of Theodosius II (408-450). This bust type was standard until the late 6th century.
2. Solidus (obverse only) of Zeno (474-491). Reverse similar to that of No. 4.
3. 40 Nummia bronze of Anastasius (491-518), Constantinople mint, small module type.
4. Solidus of Justin I (518-527). Compare obverse type with that of No. 11.
5. 40 Nummia bronze of Justinian I (527-565), Constantinople mint, year 18, 1st officina.
6. 40 Nummia bronze of Justinian I, Antioch mint, 4th officina, undated.
7. 20 Nummia bronze of Justinian I, Antioch mint, 4th officina, undated.
8. 5 Nummia bronze of Justinian I, Constantinople mint, undated.
9. 5 Nummia bronze bearing monogram of Justinian on obverse, "non-imperial" type.
10. 40 Nummia bronze of Justin II with Sophia, Constantinople mint, year 5, 4th officina.
11. Solidus of Justin II (565-578). Compare obverse with No. 4.
12. Solidus of Tiberius II Constantine (578-582). This reverse became standard for this denomination and was used with minor variations until the 8th century.
13. 10 Nummia bronze of Tiberius II, Antioch mint, year 7. No officina mark.
14. 20 Nummia bronze of Tiberius II, Antioch mint, year 2. No officina mark (see text).
15. 40 Nummia bronze of Maurice Tiberius (582-602), Constantinople mint, year 8.
16. 40 Nummia bronze of Maurice, "imperial" bust type, Nicomedia mint, year 4, 1st officina.
17. 40 Nummia bronze of Maurice, "Consular" type, Antioch mint, year 12, 3rd officina.
18. 10 Nummia bronze of Maurice, Antioch mint, year 10. No officina mark.
19. 40 Nummia bronze of Focas (602-610), Constantinople mint, 5th officina, year 2.
20. 20 Nummia bronze of Focas with Leontia, Constantinople mint, undated, 3rd officina.
21. 40 Nummia bronze of Focas with Leontia, Antioch mint, year 4. No officina mark.
22. Solidus (obverse only) of Focas. Note the characteristic beard on his bust.
23. Early solidus struck by Heraclius (610-641). Compare with No. 22.
24. Solidus of Heraclius of the "three standing Augusti" type. Note monogram on reverse.
25. 40 Nummia bronze of the type struck by Heraclius mainly between years 3 to 5. Overstruck on a 40 nummia bronze of Focas.
26. 40 Nummia bronze of Heraclius of the type struck from years 20 to 29. Note that the emperor is wearing armor while Heraclius Constantine is wearing robes.
27. 40 Nummia bronze of the type struck by Heraclius from year 6 to 19 with Martina, Heraclius, and Heraclius Constantine as the obverse types, Cyprus mint, year 17, 3rd officina. (See IERC IV, fig. 8.)
28. 12 Nummia bronze of Heraclius from the Alexandria mint with the standing figure obverse.
29. 12 Nummia bronze of Heraclius from the Alexandria mint with the two facing busts obverse.
30. Solidus of Constantine III (641-668) struck early in his reign.
31. Solidus of Constantine III struck late in his reign with his three sons.
32. 40 Nummia bronze of Constantine III, Constantinople mint, year 3. (Also see IERC IV, figs. 3 and 9.)
33. Solidus of Constantine IV (668-685) with his two brothers. (See IERC IV, fig. 4.)

34. Solidus of Constantine V (741-775) with Leo IV (son) and Leo III (father). (See fig. 12.)
35. Bronze of Leo IV (775-780) with Constantine VI (son) on the obverse face and Leo III and Constantine V (grandfather and father) on the reverse.
36. Solidus of Leo IV similar in type to No. 35.
37. Bronze of Leo V (813-820) with son Constantine. The emperor can be distinguished by the lozenge pattern of his robe.
38. Bronze ("follis") of Theophilus (829-842). (See IERC I, fig. 15.)
39. Bronze ("Half follis") of Theophilus with the new reverse type.
40. Solidus of Basil I (867-886) with son Constantine. Seated figure of Christ is the reverse type.
41. Bronze of Basil I alone.
42. Bronze of Basil I with eldest son Constantine (who died before his father).
43. Bronze of Basil I with sons Constantine and Leo (later Leo VI).
44. Rare solidus of Leo VI (886-912) with son Constantine VII.
45. Bronze of Romanus I (919-944), Constantinople mint.
46. Bronze of Romanus I from the Cherson mint with monogram obverse.
47. Bronze of Nicephorus II (963-969).
48. Anonymous bronze, Bellinger type 1. (See IERC I, fig. 21.)
49. Anonymous bronze, Bellinger type 2.
50. Anonymous bronze, Bellinger type 6.
51. Anonymous bronze, Bellinger type 9.
52. Anonymous bronze, Bellinger type 11.
53. Solidus of Theodora.
54. Scyphate gold nomisma of Isaac I (1057-1059) (obverse only). Note the drawn sword.
55. Bronze of Constantine X (1059-1067). (See IERC IV, fig. 10.)
56. Bronze of Romanus IV (1067-1071).
57. Scyphate gold nomisma of Michael VII (1071-1078).
58. Bronze of Alexius I (1081-1118) with Virgin holding medallion of Christ on the reverse face.
59. Bronze of Alexius I.
60. Bronze of Alexius I. John II struck similar coins differing mainly in the legends.
61. Scyphate gold nomisma of John II (1118-1143) with John and St. Michael on the obverse.
62. Scyphate gold nomisma of John II with facing busts of John and the Virgin on the obverse.
63. Scyphate gold nomisma of John II with standing figures of John and the Virgin on the obverse face.
64. Scyphate gold nomisma of Manuel I (1143-1180).
65. Scyphate bronze of Manuel I with the emperor and Virgin on the obverse face.
66. Scyphate bronze nomisma of Andronicus I (1183-1185) showing the emperor and Christ on the obverse face, and the Virgin as the reverse type.
67. Scyphate gold nomisma of Isaac (1185-1195) showing the emperor and St. Michael on the obverse face.
68. Small bronze of Alexius III (1195-1203) with St. George as the reverse type.

NOTES

NOTES

NOTES

NOTES

NOTES

DURST PUBLICATIONS
Offering the Best in Numismatic Books
(Including Forthcoming Titles)

We stock approximately 2000 titles relating to Coins, Medals, Paper Money, Stocks, Bonds, Tokens and other Numismatic items, in all areas of interest.

U.S.

Adams, E., UNITED STATES STORE CARDS . . . . S-$12.00
Bowen, R.L.B., OBSOLETE BANKNOTES AND SCRIP
    OF MICHIGAN . . . . H-$45.00
Bowers, D. and Ruddy J., UNITED STATES HALF CENTS . . . . S-$10.00
Bradfield, E.G., FRANKLIN IN NUMISMATICS . . . . S-$ 8.00
Breen, W., PROOF COINS STRUCK AT THE U.S. MINT . . . . S-$10.00
Browning, A.W., EARLY QUARTER DOLLARS . . . . H-$20.00
Crosby, S.S., EARLY COINS OF AMERICA . . . . H-$45.00
Durst, L.S., U.S. NUMISMATIC AUCTION CATALOGS:
    A BIBLIOGRAPHY . . . . H-$25.00
Durst, S. (ed..), PRIVATE BANKERS OF US AND CANADA . . . . S-$10.00
Durst, S.J., EARLY AMERICAN COPPERS ANTHOLOGY . . . . H-$60.00
Durst, S.J., COMPREHENSIVE GUIDE TO AMERICAN
    COLONIAL COINAGE . . . . H-$25.00
Evans, G.G., HISTORY OF THE U.S. MINT AND COINAGE . . . . H-$25.00
Fuld, G.M., GUIDE TO CIVIL WAR STORE CARDS . . . . S-$10.00
Hancock, V. & Spanbauer, L., STANDARD CATALOG
    OF U.S. COUNTERFEIT & ALTERED COINS . . . . H-$30.00
HISTORY OF THE BUREAU OF ENGRAVING
    & PRINTING . . . . H-$30.00
Kenney, E., EARLY AMERICAN MEDALLIST
    & DIE SINKERS . . . . S-$ 6.00
Kenney, E., STRUCK COPIES OF
    EARLY AMERICAN COINS . . . . S-$ 6.00
Kenney, E., SO-CALLED DOLLARS . . . . S-$ 6.00
Kliman, M., TWO CENT PIECES AND VARIETIES . . . . S-$10.00
Kosoff, A., UNITED STATES DIMES . . . . S-$10.00
Knox, J.J., UNITED STATES NOTES . . . . H-$25.00
Low, L.H., HARD TIMES TOKENS . . . . H-$20.00
Low, L., OBSERVATIONS ON COUNTERFEITING
    COINS & MEDALS . . . . S-$ 2.00
Maris, E., COINS OF NEW JERSEY . . . . S-$15.00
Miller, H.C., STATE COINAGE OF CONNECTICUT . . . . H-$25.00
Nelson, P., COINAGE OF WILLIAM WOOD . . . . S-$ 7.00
Newman, E., COLONIAL COINS OF VIRGINIA . . . . S-$15.00
Newman, E., CONTINENTAL CURRENCY OF 1776 &
    FUGIO CENT VARIETIES . . . . S-$ 6.00
Noe, S., MASSACHUSETTS SILVER COINAGE . . . . H-$35.00
Pennell, J.R., OBSOLETE BANKNOTES OF
    NORTH CAROLINA . . . . S-$ 8.00
Ryder, H., COPPER COINS OF MASSACHUSETTS . . . . S-$ 7.00
Ryder H. & Slatter, E., COLONIAL COINS OF VERMONT . . . . S-$10.00

Schmeider, T., COLLECTING AND INVESTING IN
U.S. SMALL CENTS....................................... S-$10.00
Schuckers, J.W., FINANCES & PAPER MONEY OF
THE REVOLUTIONARY WAR .... H-$15.00
Swiatek, A., WALKING LIBERTY HALF DOLLARS.. S-$10.00, .. H-$20.00
Taxay, D., U.S. MINT AND COINAGE............................ H-$35.00
Valentine, D.W., FRACTIONAL CURRENCY OF THE U.S.......... S-$10.00
Valentine, D.W., UNITED STATES HALF DIMES................. H-$35.00
White, W., SEATED LIBERTY DOLLARS .... S-$10.00, ... H-$20.00
Willem, J., U.S. TRADE DOLLAR .... S-$20.00
Wismer, D.C., OBSOLETE BANKNOTES OF NEW YORK .... S-$20.00
Wismer, D.C., OBSOLETE BANKNOTES OF OHIO .... S-$10.00
Wismer, D.C., OBSOLETE BANKNOTES OF PENNSYLVANIA...... S-$12.00

FOREIGN

Andrews, A., AUSTRALASIAN TOKENS & COINS .... H-$35.00
Betts, B., MEXICAN IMPERIAL COINAGE AND MEDALS .... S-$ 8.00
Courteau, E., COINS AND TOKENS OF NOVA SCOTIA........... S-$ 8.00
Cresswell, O.D., CHINESE CASH................................ S-$12.00
Davis, W.J., NINETEENTH CENTURY TOKEN COINAGE.......... H-$ 45.00
Durst, S.J., CONTEMPORARY WORLD GOLD COINS............. H-$10.00
Durst, L.S. & S.J., WORLD GOLD COIN VALUE GUIDE ... S-$9.00, ... H-$12.00
Durst, L.S. & S.J., WORLD SILVER COIN VALUE GUIDE... S-$9.00, ... H-$12.00
Frey, A. & Cervin, D., DATED COINAGE OF EUROPE PRIOR TO 1501... H-$30.00
Hawkins, E., SILVER COINS OF ENGLAND..................... H-$O.O.P.
Jacobs, N. & Vermeule C., JAPANESE COINAGE .... H-$25.00
Kann, E., CURRENCIES OF CHINA............................. H-$45.00
Katz, V., THOUSAND YEARS OF BOHEMIAN COINAGE (925-1929)... S-$ 8.00
Lincoln, F., CATALOG OF PAPAL MEDALS..................... S-$10.00
Munro, N.G., COINS OF JAPAN .... H-$35.00
Mort, S.R., COINS OF THE HAPSBURG EMPERORS &
RELATED ISSUES 1619-1919............................. H-$25.00
Pradeau, A., A NUMISMATIC HISTORY OF MEXICO.............. H-$25.00
Sadow, J. & Sarro, T., COINS AND MEDALS OF THE VATICAN.... H-$15.00
Severin, H.M., GOLD AND PLATINUM COINAGE OF
IMPERIAL RUSSIA... H-$25.00
Wang, Y.C., EARLY CHINESE COINAGE....................... H-$35.00

ANCIENT & MEDIEVAL

Baldwin, A., SYMBOLISM ON GREEK COINS .... H-$20.00
Baldwin, A., FACING HEADS ON ANCIENT GREEK COINS........ S-$ 8.00
Banks, F.A., COINS OF BIBLE DAYS............................ S-$16.00
Bellinger, A.R., ESSAYS ON THE COINAGE OF
ALEXANDER THE GREAT .... H-$30.00
Bellinger, A.R., SYRIAN TETRADRACHMS...................... H-$30.00
Bellinger, A.R., TROY THE COINS............................. H-$35.00

Carson, Hill, Kent, LATE ROMAN BRONZE COINAGE............. H-$25.00
Curtis, J., TETRADRACHMS OF ROMAN EGYPT .... H-$30.00
Gardner, P., CATALOG OF COINS IN THE BRITISH MUSEUM -
  SYRIA... H-$30.00
Grant, M., ANCIENT HISTORY ATLAS.......................... S-$10.00
Head, B.V., COINAGE OF LYDIA AND PERSIA .... S-$15.00
Head, B.V., HISTORIA NUMORUM.............................. H-$60.00
Icard, S., DICTIONARY OF GREEK COIN INSCRIPTIONS .... H-$45.00
Klawans, Z., OUTLINE OF ANCIENT GREEK COINS.............. S-$12.00
Klawans, Z., READING & DATING ROMAN IMPERIAL COINS...... S-$10.00
Laurence, R.H., THE MEDALS OF GIOVANNI CAVINO -
  THE PADUAN .... S-$ 6.00
Lhotka, J., MEDIEVAL BRACTATES .... S-$12.00
Lhotka, J. and Anderson P.K., MEDIEVAL IBERIAN COINAGE...... S-$15.00
Lhotka, J., INTRODUCTION TO LATE ROMAN (BYZANTINE)
  COINAGE... S-$15.00
Mattingly, H., ROMAN COINS.................................... H-$30.00
Milne, J.G., CATALOGUE OF ALEXANDRIAN COINS.............. H-$50.00
Newell, E.T., STANDARD PTOLEMAIC SILVER .... S-$ 6.00
Newell, E., ROYAL GREEK PORTRAIT COINS..................... S-$12.00
Rogers, Rev. E.M.A., HANDY GUID TO JEWISH COINS .... H-$20.00
Seltman, C., GREEK COINS....................................... H-$30.00
Starr, C., ATHENIAN COINAGE................................... H-$20.00
Sutherland, C.H.V., COINAGE OF THE ROMAN IMPERIAL POLICY... H-$25.00
Sydenham, E., THE COINAGE OF NERO.......................... H-$20.00
Sydenham, E., THE COINAGE OF THE ROMAN REPUBLIC .... H-$35.00
Sydenham, E., HISTORICAL REFERENCES TO COINS OF
  ROMAN EMPIRE.. S-$15.00
Westdal, S., DICTIONARY OF ROMAN COIN INSCRIPTIONS ...... S-$10.00
Yoeman, MONEYS OF THE BIBLE .... S-$ 8.00

ART AND CHILDREN'S BOOKS

Trusler, THE COMPLETE WORKS OF WILLIAM HOGARTH .... H-$35.00
Rackham, A., MOTHER GOOSE - facsimile ed..................... H-$11.00
Pyle, H., KING ARTHUR & HIS KNIGHTS - facsimile ed .... H-$11.00
Kipling, R., JUST SO STORIES - facsimile ed..................... H-$11.00

GENERAL

Ana, THE NUMISMATIST, 1888-1892, (THE FIRST FIVE YEARS).... H-$50.00
Durst, S., COPYRIGHT PRACTICE AND PROCEDURE.... S-$10.00, H-$15.00
Durst, S.J., INVESTOR/COLLECTOR GUIDEBOOK............... H-$15.00
Kosoff, A., ABE KOSOFF REMEMBERS ...... S-$19.50, H-$50.00 L-$150.00
Levine, E., THE GOLDEN KEY................................... H-$25.00
Lewes, T., PEMBERTON, E., Dalston, T., EARLY FORGED STAMPS
  DETECTOR.. S-$7.00, H-$10.00
Reed, F.M., ODD AND CURIOUS .... S-$7.00, H-$12.00
Reisman, D., & Durst, S.J., BUYING AND SELLING
  COUNTRY LAND... H-$19.75
Welter, G. & Schulman, H., CLEANING & PRESERVATION OF
  COINS & MEDALS.. H-$13.00
Woodward, P.H., SECRET SERVICE OF THE POST OFFICE
  DEPARTMENT .... H-$25.00

(S = softcover H = hardcovered L = leatherbound)
(* - numbered, autographed ed.)

SANFORD J. DURST

29-28 41st Avenue
Long Island City, NY 11101 U.S.A.
Telephone 718-706-0303
Dealer & Jobber Inquiries Invited